Cornwall and [illegible]
Holiday Diaries
1955-1958

Beryl Hayward
1927 - 2006

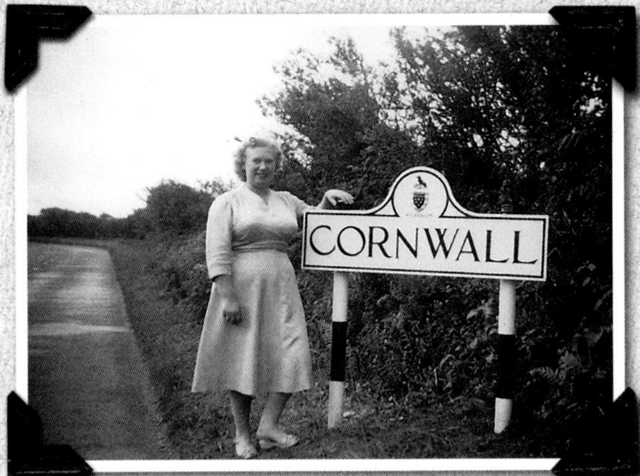
CORNWALL

Newquay and Paignton August 1955

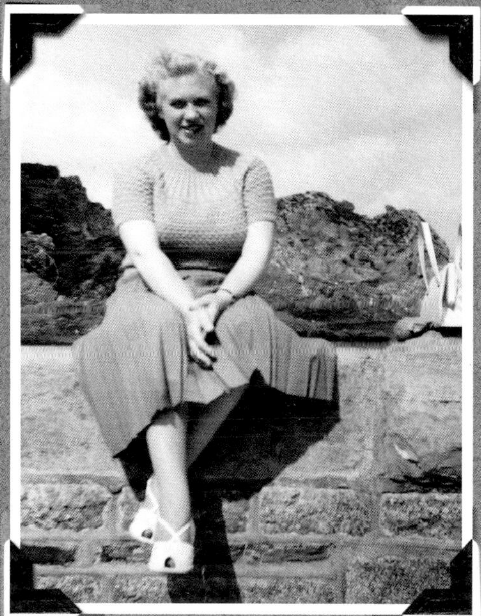

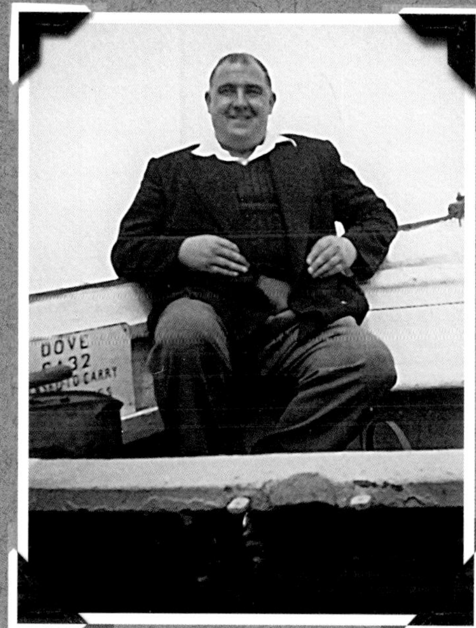

BERYL AND MAURICE

SATURDAY 20TH AUGUST

Mileage 80665 to 80900
235 miles. Petrol 7 gallons

We left Reading at 2am Saturday, and arrived at Newquay 8.10 am. Quite a good journey. Stopped once for petrol, and once for coffee and cakes. Not a terrific lot of traffic on the road, but quite a few cars parked along the hedgerows. Did not see much of the countryside until past Exeter, when it started to get light.

On arriving at Newquay we were rather disappointed with the place. It was a very dull morning and the tide was in, which made the scenery look worse. We parked the car overlooking the harbour and went to have a coffee, then walked around to get our bearings. About 11 o'clock we presented ourselves to Mrs Jeffery, a very nice person, and we were very pleased with our room.

Lunch time we had steak and kidney pies and Cornish pasties, with two light and mild and a light at the Sailor's Arms. A very tasty meal. By this time the sun was shining and everywhere looked much better. It seems that on the Friday, Newquay had had its first rain for several weeks.

In the afternoon we had a walk along the sands from Towan Beach to Lusty Glaze Beach, and took some photographs. We returned to our digs via the cliff walk.

At 6pm we had a meal, steak and chips etc. We were later to discover that it is difficult to

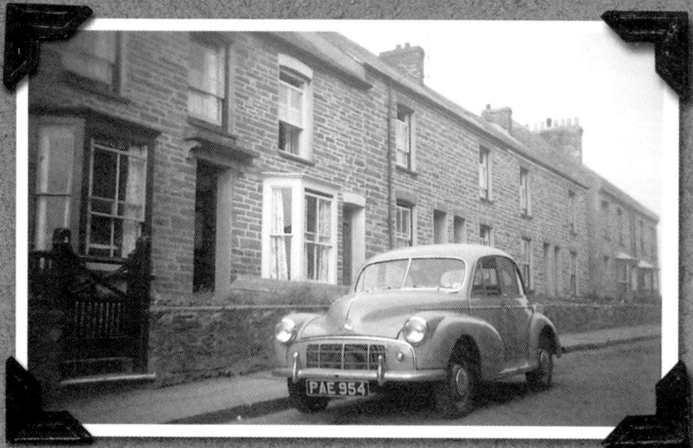

"We left Reading at 2am Saturday, and arrived at Newquay 8.10 am. Quite a good journey."

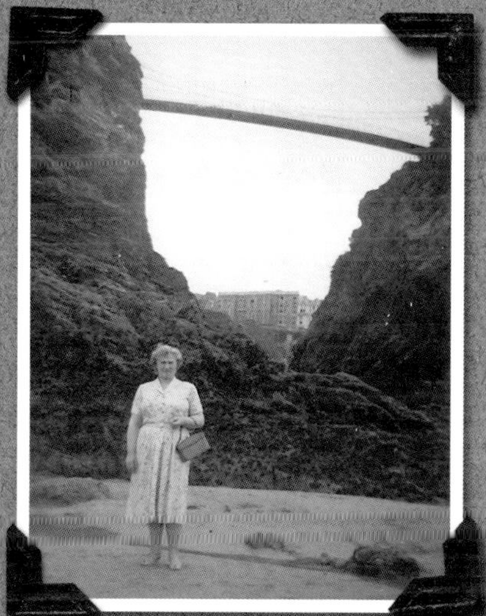

TOWAN BEACH
20 AUG 1955

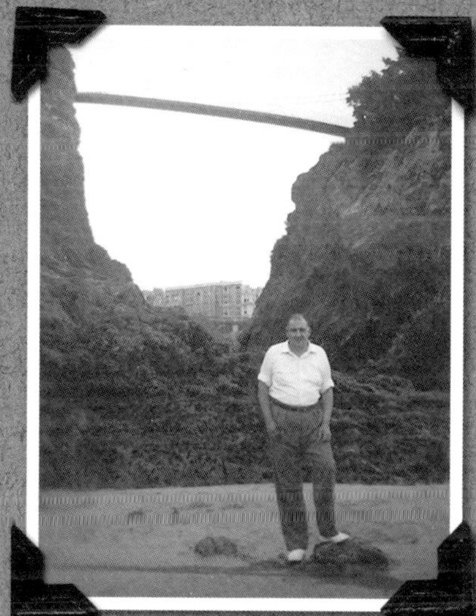

get a really good steak in Newquay. After this we set out to discover what the night life of Newquay was like. We started at the Hotel Bristol, a very sedate place, with a sherry each then made our way back to the town centre, calling at the Great Western, having a light ale each. Not such an impressive place. Next call the Central, quite a nice cocktail bar, had a port and lemon and Maury a light ale. Then we took a walk up to the Tudor bar at the Atlantic Hotel. This stands high on a cliff overlooking all Newquay, which is a very pretty view. We both had a port and lemon then returned to our digs.

This ended our first day. Considering we journeyed down overnight we were not exceptionally tired.

Sunday 21st August

Mileage 80900 to 81054
154 miles. Petrol 4 gallons

Breakfast: Cereal, bacon, egg and fried bread, toast, marmalade and tea.

At approximately 9.15 am we left Newquay to journey along the North Cornish coast as far as Clovelly. We went via Porth, Watergate Bay, Bedruthan Steps (the tide was in, so not a very impressive sight), and Wadebridge. Then on to Tintagel where we had a coffee and biscuits at King Arthur's Café before taking a walk to King Arthur's cove, which is about half a mile. We had our first bathe at this cove. It is a pebbly beach and rather sudden deep water.

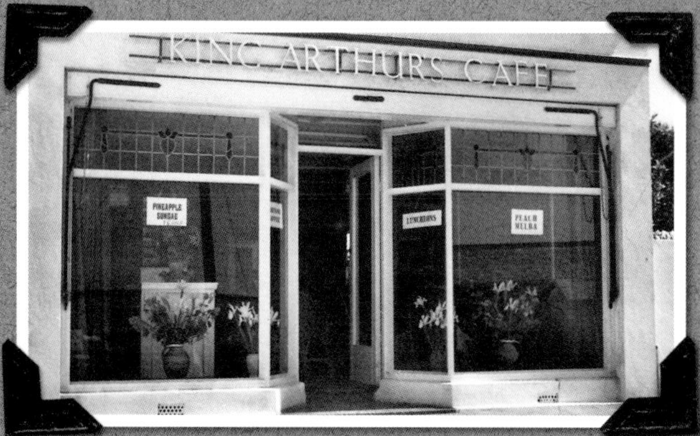

21 Aug 1955 King Arthur's Cafe, Tintagel

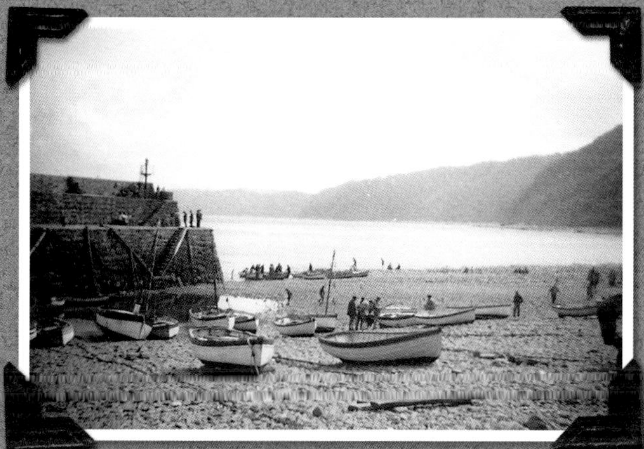

Clovelley

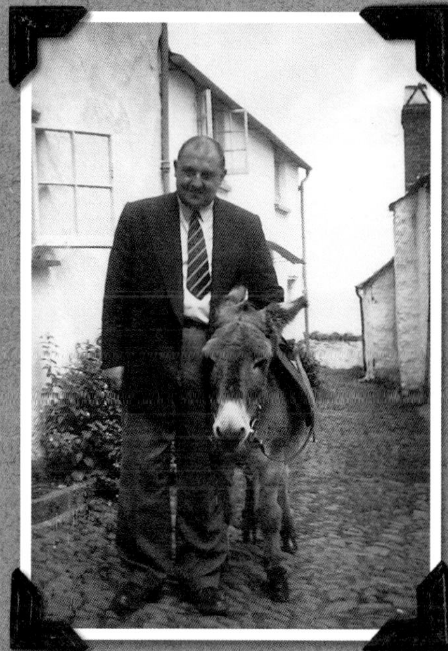

Clovelley

Had lunch at the café on the cliff top, which consisted of pea soup, roast pork, potatoes, peas, strawberries and cream and a glass of cider. After this lunch we didn't feel like walking back to the car park as it was very hot, so we rode back in a jeep.

We continued along the coast through Boscastle and Bude to Clovelly, which is, I should say, the quaintest place in that part of the country. We had to park the car and walk as there is no road for motor vehicles in this little port. We had an ice lolly then started the descent. Clovelly is actually built on the cliff face and the roadway is just a cobbled path leading down in steps to the harbour, and a very pretty sight it is when you eventually get there. The climb back is terrific, which makes you wonder whether it was worth it, but no doubt we will do the same next year! Had a well earned drink of Kia Ora, then journeyed back to Newquay via Camelford, Wadebridge etc.

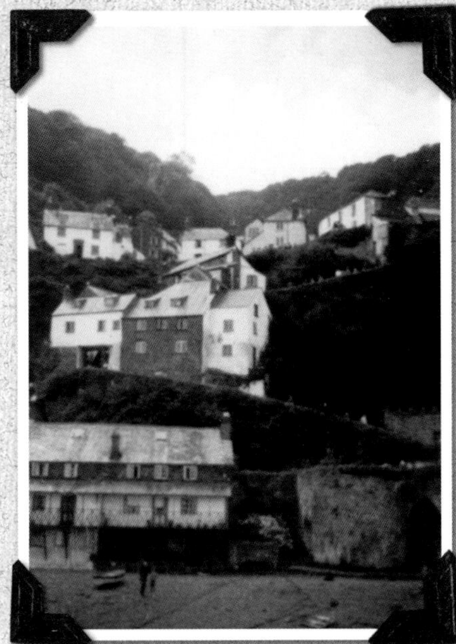

CLOVELLY
"the quaintest place"

Had a cuppa in the Cornubia before washing and changing for the evening, which we spent in Newquay. First we had a meal in the Fort Restaurant. Maurice had a farmhouse grill and I had a lamb chop and chips. Then we took a ride calling at various places on the way for a few drinks. The first stop was the Pilchard Inn (a very modern place, Lusty Glaze end of Newquay) for a light and light & mild. Next, the Bristol for two iced lagers, then St Romans in the Swiss Bar for port and lemons, then the Pentire for iced lagers. We then parked the car for the night and took a walk up to the Atlantic Tudor Bar for two Youngers bitter no 3 then gin and pineapple.

The weather today has been ideal for bathing and touring.

MONDAY 22ND AUGUST

Mileage 81054 to 81169
115 miles. Petrol 3 gallons

Breakfast: Cereal, bacon, egg and fried bread, toast, marmalade and tea.

At 9.30 we left Newquay to journey along the North Cornish coast to Land's End. Our first stop was Perranporth. Quite a nice place with a few good shops and beautiful sands. After a walk round we journeyed on to Portreath, then we came to a beautiful spot called Hell's Mouth. We took some photos here as the coastal scenery was magnificent.

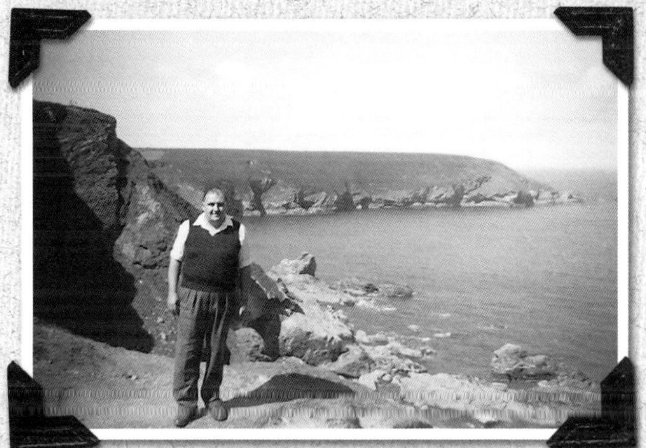

HELL'S MOUTH

Our next stop was Hayle. Not anything exceptional in the town, but the beaches here are just the job. We spent a couple of hours bathing. The surf is not quite as high as Newquay, and once beyond it we could swim easily without getting out of our depth. We had a cup of tea and a fruit tart then carried on to St Ives. This is a place we really must spend more time at next year. The harbour and town looked very quaint and the beaches looked fine for bathing, but we had already bathed and wanted to carry on to Land's End, so did not spend a lot of time here.

The day was perfect for Land's End. The sun shone, and it was so clear we were able to see the lighthouse. In fact you can just see the outline of it in the photos we took.

The roads from St Ives to Land's End were extremely narrow and the countryside is just what one would expect in Cornwall. Very rugged, with a lot of rock formations. Actually, I expected to find more of this type of countryside than we did. We returned to Newquay via Penzance, Camborne and Blackwater.

Had a cup of tea and a sandwich at the Harbour Café in Newquay before washing and changing for the evening.

Went to Trenance Gardens to take some snaps, then made our usual tour of Newquay for a few drinks. First stop, the Bristol Hotel for two iced lagers, then the Pilchard Inn for two port and lemon. Then we parked the car and took a walk to the Tudor Bar at the Atlantic Hotel for two Youngers no 3, light and mild and then Worthington Watneys bitter. Next to the Central for two light ales and then to the New Inn for a port and lemon.

So ended another day.

"First stop, the Bristol Hotel for two iced lagers, then the Pilchard Inn for two port and lemon. Then we parked the car and took a walk to the Tudor Bar at the Atlantic Hotel for two Youngers no 3, light and mild and then Worthington Watneys bitter. Next to the Central for two light ales and then to the New Inn for a port and lemon."

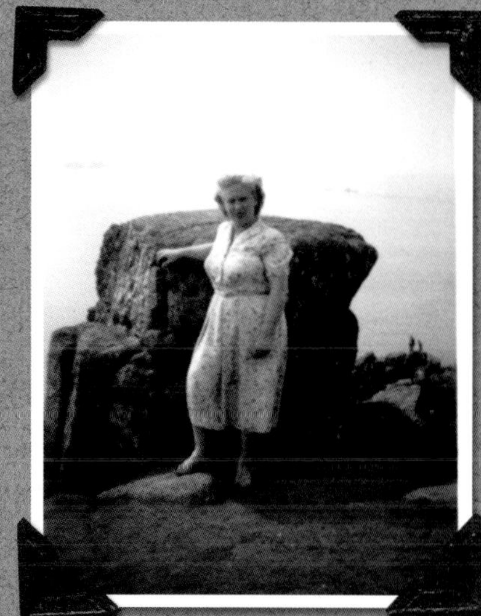

LAND'S END

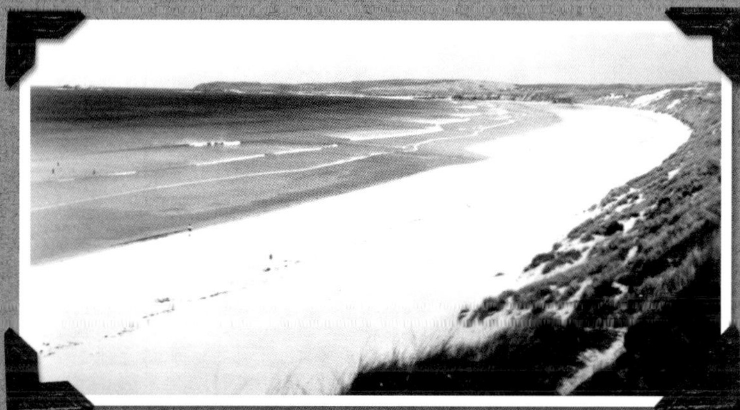

HAYLE SAND DUNES

Tuesday 23rd August

Mileage 81169 to 81285
116 miles. Petrol 4 gallons

Breakfast: Grapefruit. Sausage, bacon, tomatoes, toast, marmalade and tea.

We left Newquay at 9.30 for Penzance, quite a large town for this part of the country. We had a look round the shops and bought some rolls, tomatoes and cheese, to have for our lunch. There is a small promenade here, and an extremely good bathing pool. Newlyn Bay and Mousehole are two very quaint little harbours near Penzance.

We then made our way to Praa Sands to have our daily bathe, passing through Marazion and seeing St Michael's Mount from all angles. The best view is from the East side. After our bathe we had lunch on the beach then journeyed on to the Lizard Point via Helston.

You have to park the car and walk about a mile before you actually come to Lizard Point and it is well worth the walk. Unlike Land's End it is not cluttered with stalls selling post cards etc, and of course no car parks. We walked right round Lizard Point by a cliff path, about 3 miles in all by the time we got back to the village, where we had a well earned ice cream. I consider the coastal scenery at the Lizard far superior to that of Land's End.

Our next stop was Mullion Cove, a really picturesque harbour, which is being restored by the National Trust. The rocks form a natural haven, which affords only a small entrance to the harbour. We then returned to Newquay via Helston, Camborne and Redruth.

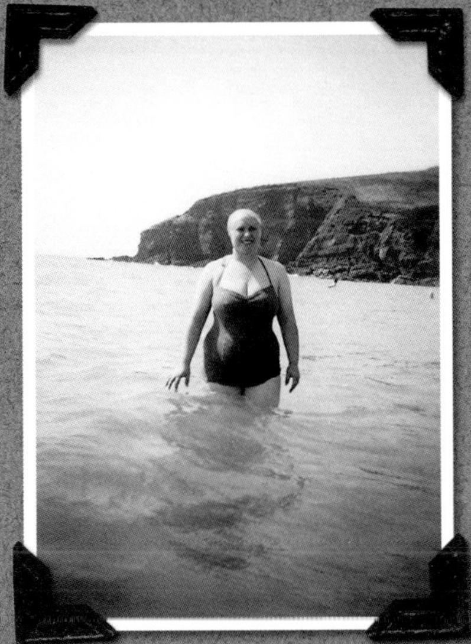

“We then made our way to Praa Sands to have our daily bathe, passing through Marazion and seeing St Michael’s Mount from all angles.”

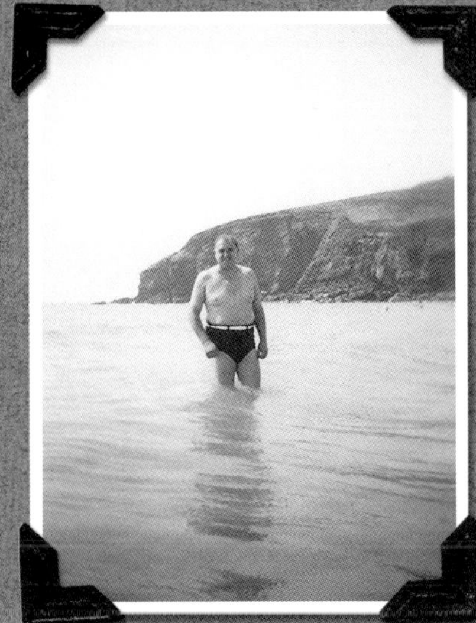

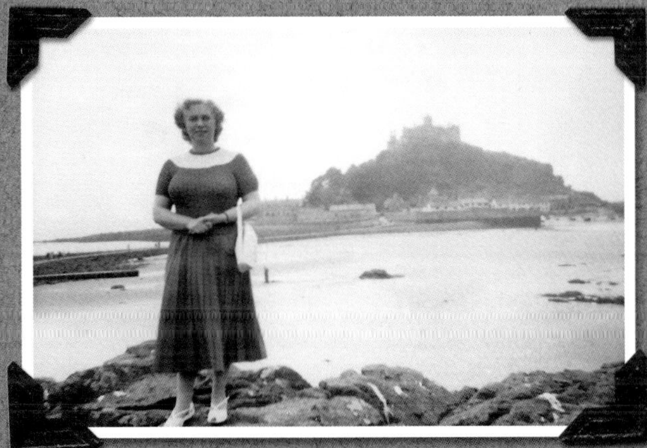

ST MICHAEL’S MOUNT

Today has been rather tiring as we have done quite a lot of walking, so after freshening up we called at the Sailor's Arms for 2 steak and kidney pies and drinks – light ale, then light and mild. Then to the Bristol for 2 iced lagers, finishing up at the Harbour Café for a cup of coffee.

Most evenings we walked down to Newquay harbour to see the lights round the top of the cliffs. Newquay isn't illuminated much, but it is a pretty sight at dusk, as the way the coast curves gives the impression that you are looking at it from the sea.

WEDNESDAY 24TH AUGUST

Mileage 81285 to 81442
157 miles. Petrol 4 gallons

Breakfast: Cereal, cold ham, hard boiled egg, toast, marmalade and tea.

Today we made a return trip to Tintagel via Wadebridge, to explore the castle. We walked up and down the 115 and 100 steps twice. Marvellous view from the cliff top. The very rugged coastline makes one wonder how they managed to build a castle there in the old days. Wouldn't like to do this walk on a windy day. We returned to the village and had a pineapple drink and ice cream at King Arthur's Café.

We then had another look at Boscastle and retuned to Wadebridge. Had a walk up the main street, not much of a place. Partook of a pint of milk and 1 lb of peas then returned to

Newquay for a bathe, which we took on Towan beach for about two hours.

We then retuned to our digs for a wash and change and then walked to Trenance Gardens to take some more photos. Then we had a meal at the Riviera café, steak, tomatoes, chips, bread & butter and tea, before having a run out to the Jamaica Inn at Bolventor. We took some photos but the light was fading and they were impossible to develop. We had a light and bitter plus a port and lemon each before returning to Newquay. Called at the Bristol for two iced lagers, then put the car away and walked up to the Tudor Bar at the Atlantic for two light ales. We finished the day with tea and corned beef sandwiches at the Harbour Café.

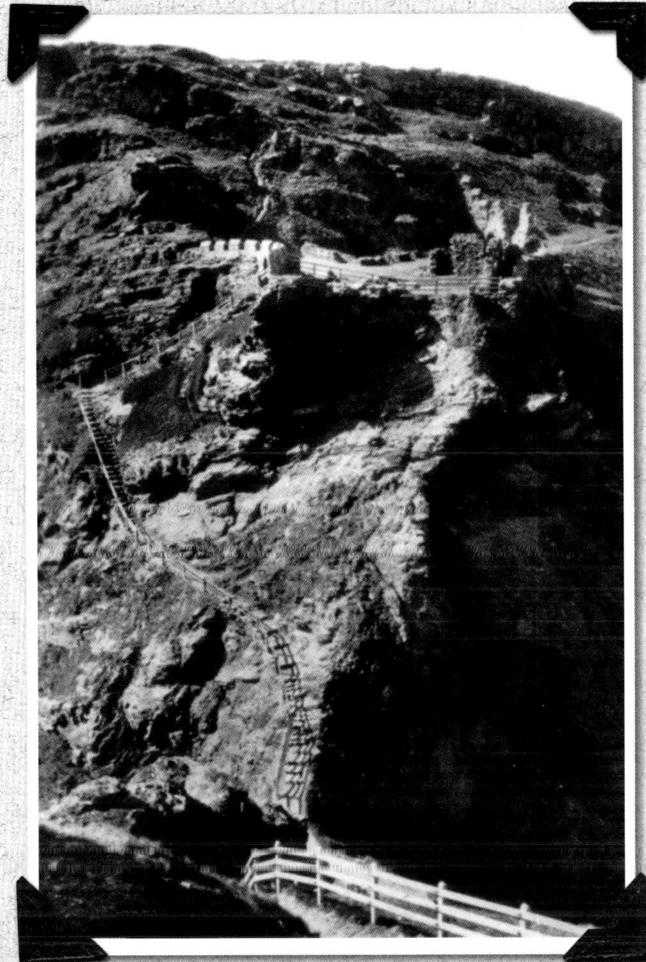

TINTAGEL STEPS

Thursday 25th August

Mileage 81442 to 81542
100 miles. Petrol 3 gallons

Breakfast: Cereal, bacon, egg, fried bread, toast, marmalade and tea.

Today we started by journeying across Cornwall from Newquay to Truro. We stopped here. Truro is nothing exceptional. The shopping centre is quite good and there is a cathedral here, but we didn't stop to have a look inside. We then carried on to Penryn and Falmouth.

Falmouth has quite a good shopping centre and a very big harbour, with a lot of ships coming and going. The beaches here are nice for bathing, but rather crowded owing to size and quite a lot of rock formation.

Gorran Haven was a nice little beach, through Portmellon and on to Mevagissey, which is a very picturesque and quaint little port. We parked the car on the jetty and had a walk around. It was rather late but we hadn't lunched, so we called at a little café and had the most delicious plaice and chips, bread and butter and a cup of tea. Just the sort of meal one would expect in such a quaint place. We then made our way back to Newquay via St Austell.

Back at Newquay we went for a most invigorating bathe on Fistral Beach. The surf is really high on the beach, so swimming is practically impossible. We spent quite a while here in the water and playing on the sands, as there is such a big expanse that you can have a good time running around playing with a beach ball.

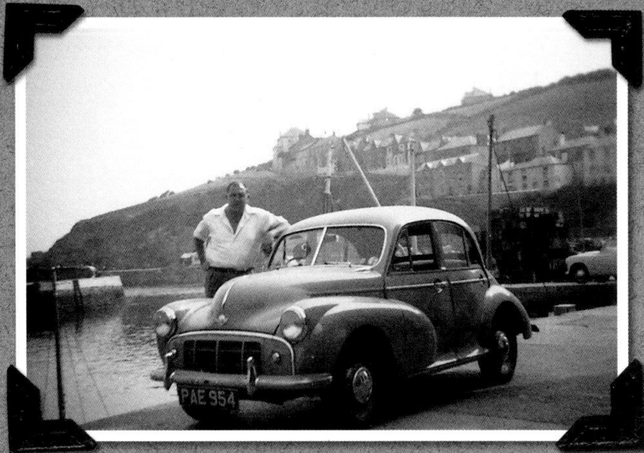

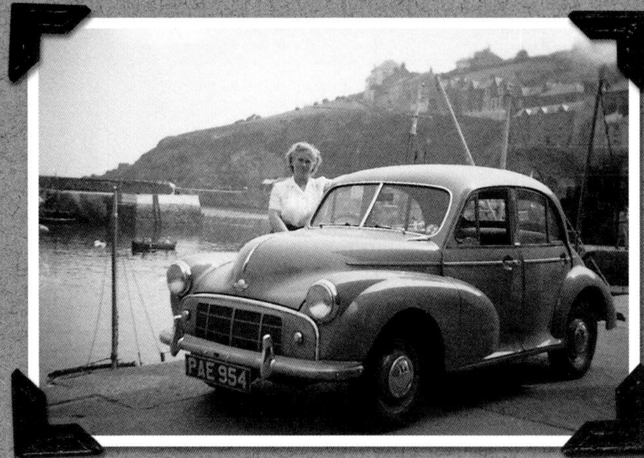

MEVAGISSEY

"We called at a little café and had the most delicious plaice and chips, bread and butter and a cup of tea. Just the sort of meal one would expect in such a quaint place."

In the evening we had a walk and called at the Pilchard for large and small shandys, the Bristol for two iced lagers and the Tudor bar for two light ales. We then had a meal at the the Cadoc Restaurant consisting of steak, chips, peas, bread and butter and tea.

So ended another day. The weather conditions are still ideal for a perfect holiday.

FRIDAY 26TH AUGUST

Mileage 81542 to 81676
134 miles. Petrol 3 gallons

Breakfast: Grapefruit, sausage, egg, tomato, toast, marmalade and tea.

Our first call today was Looe which we journeyed to via Bodmin. We found quite a lot to interest us at Looe. The shopping centre was quite good and the scenery very pretty. It was a pleasant sight to watch the boats in and out of the harbour. We had a good bathe here, as it was ideal for swimming, the only trouble being to find somewhere to get dressed as the beaches are very small. We ended up driving out and finding a quiet place to dry and dress in comfort, then went back to Looe for a meal at the Duchy Café. Cod, chips, bread and butter and tea. Before leaving we paid a visit to the Rabbitry and saw some really marvellous rabbits!

Then on to Polperro, a very quaint place, but absolutely crowded with sightseers. In view of this we didn't stay long and made our way to Fowey.

Fowey is a very nice place. We had a look around and visited the Aquarium, which was quite good. We then made our way back to Newquay.

In the evening we had a ride out to Perranporth, stopped and had a breather, also a drink. We had a light ale and a pint of bitter and watched a game of skittles, then back to Newquay, calling at the Pilchard Inn for two gin and pineapples, the Bristol for two iced lagers, the Pentire for two light ales, St Roman's Swiss bar for two gin and grapefruits and finished at the Tudor Bar with one Watneys, one Youngers and two gin and grapefruits. Before returning for the night we had a snack at the Harbour Café. Corned beef and tomato sandwiches, tea and garribaldi biscuits. Lastly a walk down to the harbour.

Another glorious day of our holiday over. This finished the part of our holiday at Newquay. Apart from the first few hours, we were very impressed with all we saw and resolved to spend a further holiday there to explore more fully the magnificent coastline, quaint harbours and coves.

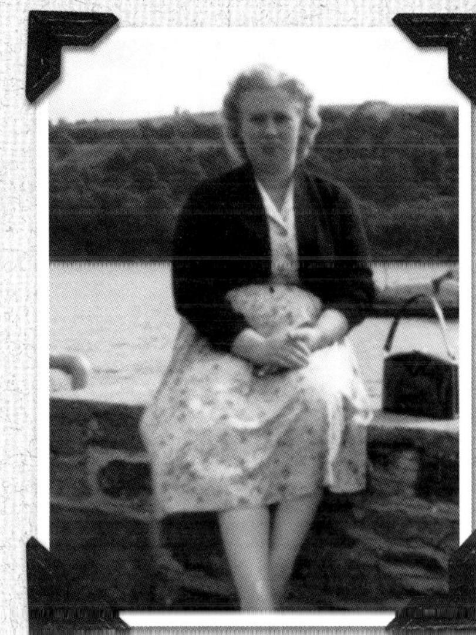

FOWEY

Saturday 27th August

Mileage 81676 to 81802
126 miles. Petrol 4 gallons

Breakfast: Cereal, bacon, egg, fried bread, toast, marmalade and tea.

Today we started the second part of our holiday which meant leaving Newquay directly after breakfast, and making for Paignton, a journey of about 90 miles. Our route took us through Bodmin, Tavistock and Totnes, which of course took us right across Dartmoor, which we considered really beautiful scenery. We did not stop to explore any of the beauty spots, but promised ourselves a whole day to tour the moor later in the week.

We arrived at the Waterside Hotel at Three Beaches about noon, and after booking in we had lunch here. Fruit juice, beef salad, rhubard and custard. In the afternoon we explored the shopping centre of Torquay and walked out on the pier and quay. Then we returned to the Waterside to have a rest, as the journey from Newquay was rather tiring.

In the evening we fortified ourselves with a drink, two lights plus light and mild, at the Waterside, then took a ride out to Brixham. This is quite a nice little place, especially the three coves at Fishcombe which is nearby. We then went back to Torquay which is very pretty indeed at night with the illuminations. We had two light ales at the Exeter, then parked the car and took a walk. We called at the Belgrave for gin and pineapples, and the Nile bar for gin and grapefruits. After our walk we returned to the Waterside, had a brown and velvet and gin and grapefruit, then went over to the café opposite for a cheese and tomato

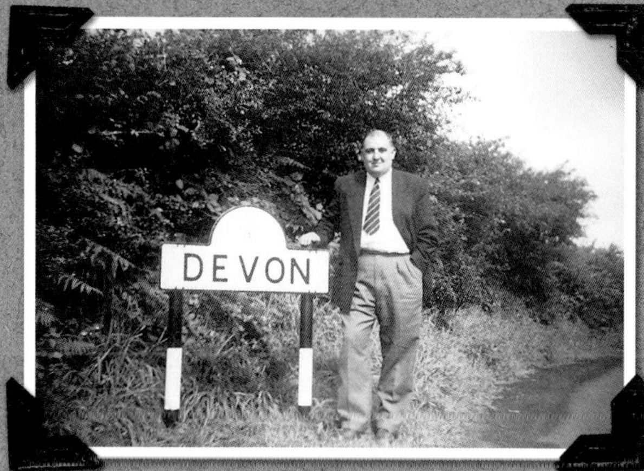

"Since being in Devon we
have found our appetites..."

sandwich and tea before retiring for the night.

Not exactly struck with Paignton. Torquay is quite nice, but unfortunately the hotel we are staying at is some distance away, and it will mean we will have to use the car evenings as well as during the day. The Waterside Hotel is not a bad sort of place to stay at, but rather rowdy at night.

Sunday 28th August

Mileage 81802 to 81927
125 miles. Petrol 4 gallons

Breakfast: Orange juice, poached egg on toast, toast and marmalade and tea.

Spent the day touring Dartmoor via Totnes and Buckfast Abbey, which is a most beautiful building. We took some photos and moved on to Buckfastleigh, Holne, Ashburton, Bovey Tracey and Widecombe, the quaintest little place imaginable where we had a glass of real cider at the Olde Inne.

Then on to Haytor, where we parked the car and climbed to the top of the tor. It doesn't look very steep, but quite a climb all the same, though the view from the top was marvellous. There is rolling moorland as far as the eye can see and we took some photos, before journeying on to Moretonhampstead.

We had a very nice home cooked lunch of steak and kidney pie, potatoes, carrots, beans,

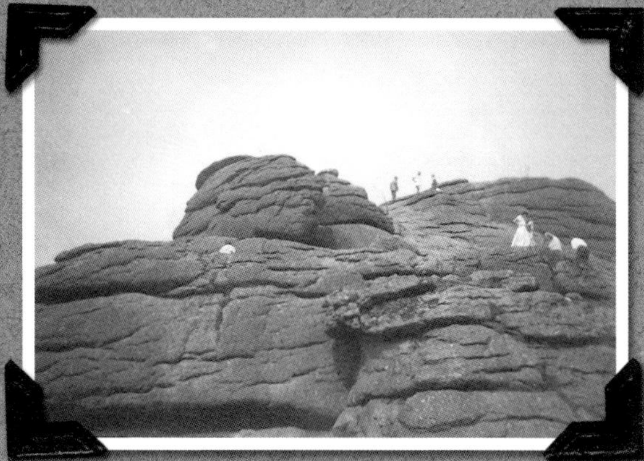

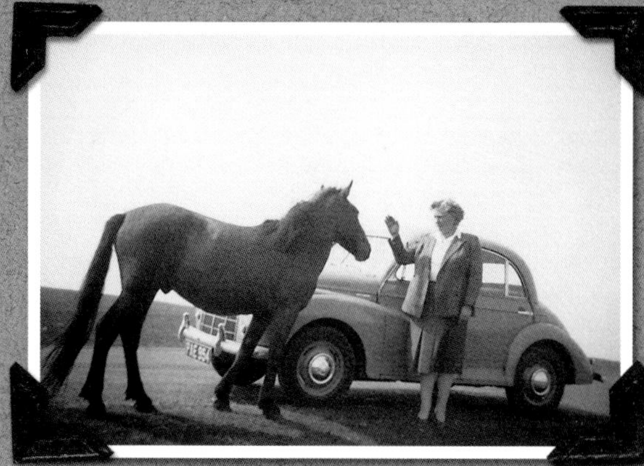

DARTMOOR

"It doesn't look very steep, but quite a climb all the same, though the view from the top was marvellous."

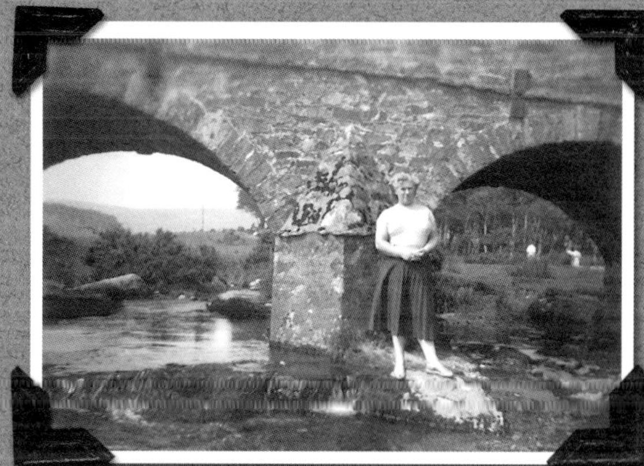

plums and custard and tea at the Alexandra Café. We then carried on to Post Bridge, a well known beauty spot, and then to Princetown, which is a very grey looking place but with lots of ponies in the Market Square. Next place Tavistock and then back to Paignton via Two Bridges, Ashburton and Totnes.

Back at Paignton we took a walk down to Goodrington Sands, which are the nearest beaches to the hotel. They were very crowded as the tide was in.

In the evening we explored Torquay and District still further. Daddyhole Plain is a good spot for an uninterrupted view of coastline. Ansteys Cove, Babbacombe and Oddicombe looked quite nice beaches, but a terrific climb. We returned to Torquay for a walk and a few drinks. We had iced lagers in the Gibbons Hotel lounge bar and sherries in the cocktail lounge. Two light ales in the Yacht Hotel and gin and grapefruits in the lounge of the Mayflower. Since being in South Devon we have "found" our appetites and fortunately, a good restaurant called the Chicken Grill, where we had supper consisting of fried steak, peas, chips and tomatoes, bread and butter and tea.

We then returned to the Waterside via Paignton sea front, which is also illuminated very well and rather unusual. Finished the day with a port and lemon each.

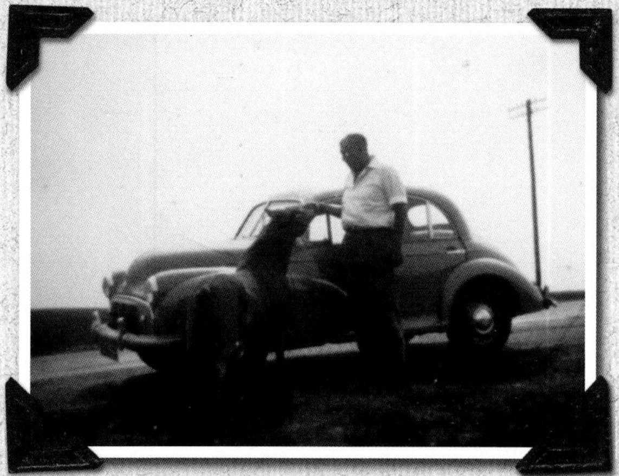

DARTMOOR

Monday 29th August

Mileage 81927 to 82058
131 miles. Petrol 3 gallons

Breakfast: Cornflakes, bacon and egg, toast, marmalade and tea.

Our first objective today after leaving Paignton was Plymouth. The ride was not all that interesting. Plymouth will eventually be a fine city, and there is indeed a beautiful shopping centre there, but still a great deal of demolition work and building has to be carried out before it is finished. We took a walk round the shops and on to the Hoe. We went to the top of the tower from where we had a beautiful view of the gardens and out to sea. We then toured the docks area, but were unable to see any ships at close quarters.

We called at the Jamaica Inn (what a dump) for two light ales. We really wanted cider, but it appears they are not allowed to sell it. We then went to the Crystal Bar at the Great Western Hotel for two more light ales, before having lunch. Both of these places were typical of the type of bar one would expect to find in a large port near the docks area. At the Excelsior Café we partook of oxtail soup, steak and kidney pudding, roast and boiled potatoes, peas and butter beans, followed by apple tart with custard and tea. We then

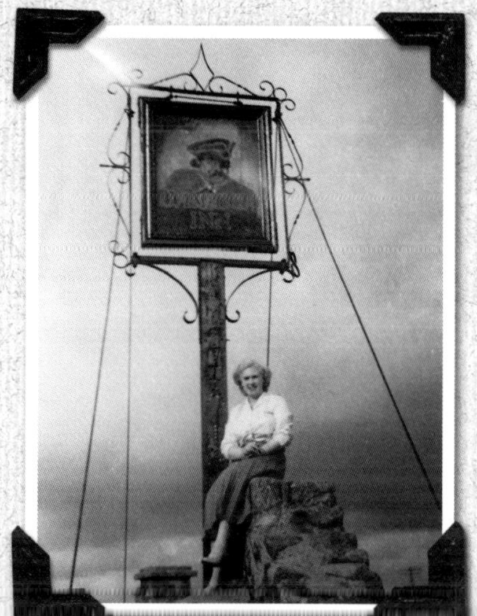

Jamaica Inn

returned to Paignton passing through Newton Ferrers, a very quaint place on the River Yealm, Salcombe, which was very nice, Kingsbridge and Totnes.

In the evening we went into Torquay and took a walk on the pier, taking photos of ourselves with the harbour in the background. There are some fine little craft in Torquay harbour. Then we returned to Paignton and had a walk round Goodrington Cliffs, which affords quite a pretty view. We had a few drinks in Paignton and found the bars far superior in the way of decoration to any we had so far come across. We had a gin and grapefruit in the Old Barn bar of the Hydro Hotel, a marvellous place, with dancing and music nightly. Two lagers at the casino, photos of which are in the large album, then we returned to the Hydro Hotel and visited Drakes Bar for a sherry each. The most outstanding feature in the bars at the Hydro is the beautiful wood carvings.

Back to Torquay for our supper, calling first at Gibbons lounge bar for a lager. We then made our way to the Chicken Grill for fried steak, chips, peas, tomatoes, bread and butter, and a cup of tea.

I may have mentioned before that we found it very difficult to get a good meal in Newquay. Fortunately our appetites were poor there, but we are making up for it here every night as the food is delicious.

"Our next stop was Kingswear from where we had a lovely view across the River Dart to Dartmouth. The Naval College is an impressive sight."

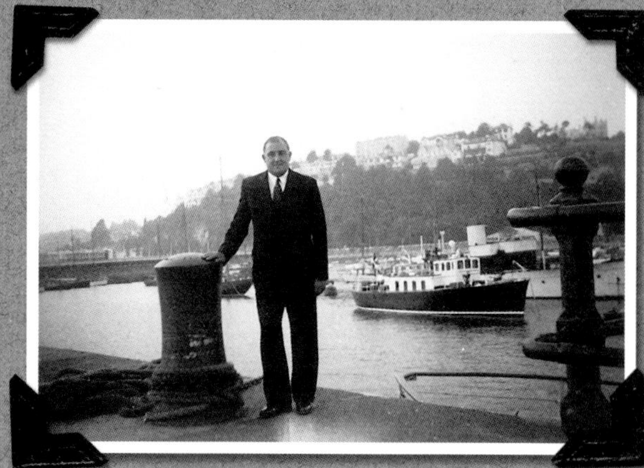

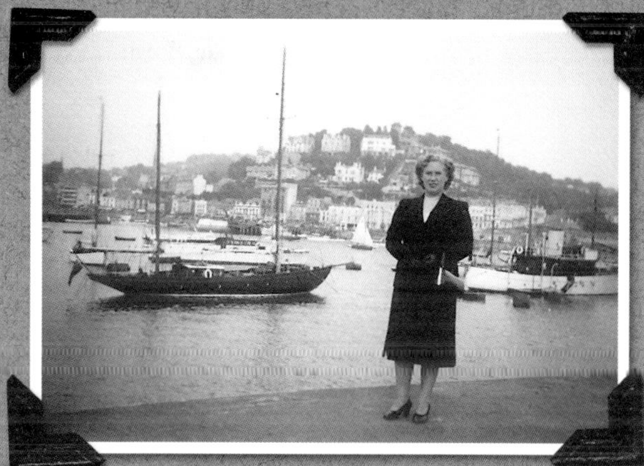

DARTMOUTH

TUESDAY 30TH AUGUST

Mileage 82058 to 82140
82 miles. Petrol 3 gallons

Breakfast: Cornflakes, bacon and egg (Maurice), haddock (Beryl), toast, marmalade and tea.

We paid a return visit to Brixham this morning, and arrived in time to see the daily catch of fish being loaded for transportation elsewhere. It was a worthwhile sight to see all the gulls having a good feed. Our next stop was Kingswear, from where we had a lovely view across the River Dart to Dartmouth. The Naval College is an impressive sight.

Next stop Totnes. Although we have passed through here several times, we haven't had a proper look round, so did so this morning. We had also been through Kingsbridge, so did the same there, then carried on to Torcross. This is a rather unusual sort of place, no harbour, but a lovely stretch of shingle beach. We had lunch at Torcross; tomato soup, roast beef, roast and boiled potatoes, peas, carrots, fruit and custard, and lemon squash.

After lunch we took the coast road to Dartmouth, quite a pleasant ride. Dartmouth is a very nice little port. We took a ride out to the castle, and saw some really beautiful river mouth scenery. Then returned to Paignton via the Dartmouth river ferry. Visited Paignton Zoo. Quite a few large animals there, such as the cat family, but the surroundings are not at all pleasant, rather smelly too.

We returned to the hotel for a bath, which after visiting the zoo we felt we needed. Dressed to go out for another pleasant evening, which we started by having two and a half lagers in the the Tyrolean Bar at the Waterside. We then rode out to Cockington Village, an old world place, about two miles from Torquay. We had a very pleasant walk in the park there, round the lakes. It's very pretty indeed, quiet and peaceful, and we then made our way back to the village, where we had two lagers in the Drum Inn.

Returned to Torquay for our usual evening tour of the popular bars, had two lagers in the Royal lounge, and then two gin and grapefruits in the Mayflower cocktail bar. We then visited the Chicken Grill for a mixed grill consisting of beef steak for Maurice, and lamb chops for Beryl: chips, bacon, egg, sausage, tomatoes, peas and liver. Tea, bread and butter.

So, ended another full and happy day. We are certainly taking advantage of the perfect weather conditions, and seeing as much of the delightful countryside as possible.

WEDNESDAY 31ST AUGUST

Mileage 82140 to 82243
103 miles. Petrol 3 gallons

Breakfast: Cornflakes, bacon, egg, toast, marmalade and tea.

This morning it was dull, the first time since the commencement of our holiday, but it soon brightened up. Our first stop was Newton Abbot, a nice little town. We had a walk round then carried on to Exeter, which we thought a very pleasant City indeed, beautiful shopping centre and good suburban districts on the by-pass. We bought a photo album and diary in Exeter.

After a good walk round and a snack in Marks & Spencer, a glass of milk and cake, we journeyed on to Exmouth, another very pleasant seaside resort, with a good beach. From there to Teignmouth via Starcross, where we saw a lovely view of Exmouth, also passing through Dawlish. At Teignmouth we had a bathe. Quite a good beach, and though the sea was rather choppy, we enjoyed it nevertheless. Of course, there was the usual problem of where to dress, and we had to take a ride out. Maurice hadn't got his sandals and as his feet were rather sandy, he drove without shoes. We eventually parked and dressed in a field with high hedges, then returned to Teignmouth to have a walk around before returning back to Paignton.

After washing and dressing for the evening we had a light ale and light and mild in the Tyrolean Bar before once again setting forth for the evening. Rode into Torquay, then had a walk around, visiting the following places on the way. The lounge bar of the Abbey Hotel for two light ales, and the Nile Bar of the Torbay Hotel for two more light ales. The lounge bar of Gibbons for two iced lagers and two more iced lagers in the Mayflower lounge, before having our supper in the Chicken Grill. Steak, liver, sausage, egg, chips, peas, tomatoes and bacon. Tea, bread and butter, after which we returned to Paignton, parked the car and took a walk.

Went into the Old Barn bar at the Hydro Hotel for two gin and grapefruits, before strolling down to the harbour. The illuminations of Torbay looked very pretty indeed from this angle. We had a light ale each in the Harbour Inn, which I might add was a very lovely place, then returned to the Waterside for a night cap, port and lemon in the Sherry Bar, before returning for the night.

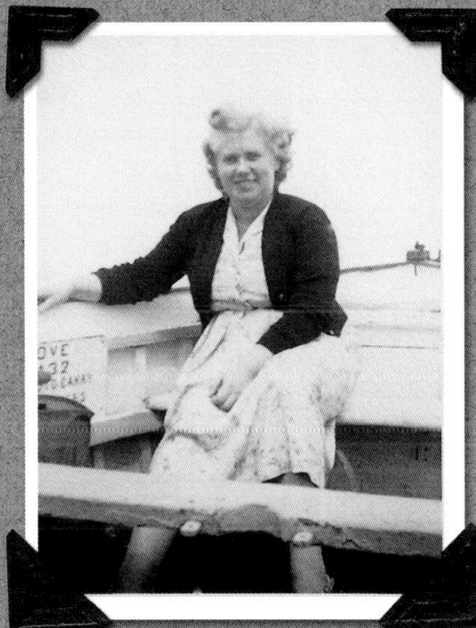

"Of course, there was the usual problem of where to dress, and we had to take a ride out. Maurice hadn't got his sandals and as his feet were rather sandy, he drove without shoes. We eventually parked and dressed in a field with high hedges, then returned to Teignmouth to have a walk around before returning back to Paignton."

THURSDAY 1ST SEPTEMBER

Mileage 82243 to 82404
161 miles. Petrol 4 gallons

Breakfast: Cornflakes, kippers, toast, marmalade and tea.

This morning Torbay looked perfect, a beautiful clear sunny morning. Our objective was Lyme Regis, just inside the Dorset boundary, so as it was some distance to go we journeyed straight there via Newton Abbot and Exeter. Before entering Lyme Regis we had a marvellous view of the coastline. Lyme Regis is nothing special, rather hilly. We had a walk along the front and called at the Mad Hatters café for coffee, before making our way back along the coast.

We called at Seaton and Sidmouth, both of which are nothing to write home about, pebbly beaches, then on to Branscombe, a very quaint village just off the coast. The beach is some distance away, this too was pebbly. Maurice had a bathe, but I stayed on the water's edge as the sea was quite choppy and it got deep very quickly. From here we went to Budleigh Salterton, just another ordinary little resort, then on to Exmouth where we had a really good bathe. It wasn't very sunny, but the sea was quite warm and the beach was sandy. We had tea at the Mocha Café, plaice and chips, bread, butter and tea. Very nice. We then returned to Paignton.

The weather seems to be on the change, it has been rather overcast at times today, and a light drizzle has started. I hope it will clear up, as it would be such a shame not to be able to have our daily bathe.

After dressing for the evening we had a light ale and light and mild in the Tyrolean Bar. We then took a ride to Brixham, parked the car and walked around. Brixham by night is not much of a place, the entertainment is poor. I guess most people go into Torquay for the evening. We had a double diamond and light ale and mild in the Bolton, then walked down to the harbour and had two gin and golds in the Butlers Arms, quite a smart little place, then returned to Paignton.

We had two double diamonds in the Gerston, then two and one iced lagers in the casino, two double diamonds in the Coronation Bar of the Esplanade Hotel, and two gin and grapefruits in the wardroom of the Redcliffe Hotel. This is a nice bar, done out like a ship, and we have a photo of it in the large album. After our 'pub crawl' we went into Torquay for our usual supper at the Chicken Grill, steak, liver, sausages, egg, chips, peas, tomatoes, bacon, bread, butter and tea.

I am very pleased to say the drizzle did not last, and we had a lovely fine evening.

Friday 2nd September

Mileage 82404 to 82504
100 miles. Petrol 3 gallons

Breakfast: Poached egg on toast, toast, marmalade and tea.

Our first stop today was Bigbury on Sea, which we reached via Totnes. The beach and view of the coastline here is beautiful. When the tide is out it is possible to walk across the sands to Burgh Island, ideal for bathing, but unfortunately we arrived here rather early and it wasn't all that warm. We had a coffee in the Burgh Island Beach Café, then carried on to Thurlestone, a very picturesque village with mainly thatched houses, but the beach here is not quite so nice.

Next stop Salcombe. We had been here before but stopped and had another walk around. The tide was out so it wasn't very suitable for bathing. In view of this we returned to Paignton and took a bathe from Goodrington Sands. It hadn't been too sunny today, but it did manage to shine whilst we were bathing.

We returned to the hotel to bath and dress ready for the evening. We then visited the

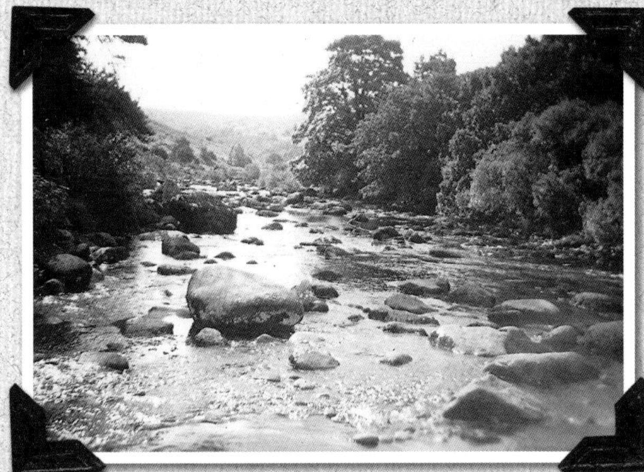

Dartmoor

Chicken Grill for fried beef steak, chips, peas, tomatoes, bread and butter and tea. Then went along to Kents Caverns to have a look at the caves. They were very impressive, not so delicate as Cheddar, but very natural and quite large. We then returned to the harbour area of Torquay, parked the car, and started out for our usual round of drinks with one and two iced lagers at the lounge bar of the Gibbons, two more lagers at the Mayflower, then took a walk as far as Marine Spa, and back to Gibbons for two gin and pineapples.

We then took a ride back to Paignton, calling at the Wardroom Bar of the Redcliffe Hotel for two lagers. We then parked the car and had a walk around a few of the side roads of the seafront, looking in the shop windows, and called at the Gerston cocktail bar for two port and lemons. Next stop was the Old Barn Bar at the Hydro Hotel for two gin and grapefruits, then we took a walk along the seafront, stopping at the casino for two lagers. We then drove into Torquay to the Chicken Grill for our supper. Liver, tomatoes, peas, chips, bread, butter and tea.

Then home to bed, home being the Waterside Hotel of course!

SATURDAY 3RD SEPTEMBER

Mileage 82504 to 82628
124 miles. Petrol 3 gallons

Breakfast: Kippers (Maurice), poached egg on toast (Beryl), toast, marmalade and tea.

As this was the last day of our holiday we made our farthest trip in Devon, a ride across Dartmoor. Our route took us through some very narrow lanes and we saw some beautiful scenery. Newton Abbot, Lustleigh, Mortonhampstead, Chagford, Two Bridges, Widecombe, Buckland and Ashburton, where we had lunch at Barnes Café. Roast beef, Yorkshire pudding, roast and boiled potatoes and runner beans. Apple tart, custard and a cup of tea. This was a very nicely cooked meal.

We then made our way to Teignmouth to have a bathe. The sea was very warm once we were in and not quite so choppy as yesterday. We stayed in the water for about an hour, then returned to Paignton to dress ready for the evening.

We had a light ale and light and mild in the Tyrolean Bar, then went to the Coverdale Hotel, which is another Simonds hotel, for the same again, plus chicken sandwiches. Then we took a ride out to Newton Abbot to the Penguin for two double diamonds, back to Torquay to Gibbons lounge for two iced lagers, then the Abbey Hotel for two more iced lagers. Back to Gibbons for two gin and grapefruit, these were extra nice with ice and a slice of lemon. We then took a trip into Paignton to visit the Wardroom at the Redcliffe Hotel for two iced lagers, and the Old Barn Bar at the Hydro Hotel for two gin and grapefruits after which we returned to Torquay. We had our supper at the Chicken Grill, fried steak, liver, sausages, bacon, peas, eggs, chips, tomatoes, bread, butter and tea.

So ended our holiday. Tomorrow we return home, taking with us some delightful memories and wonderful photographs of the places we have visited. Maurice had a beautiful suntan and I didn't do so bad myself!

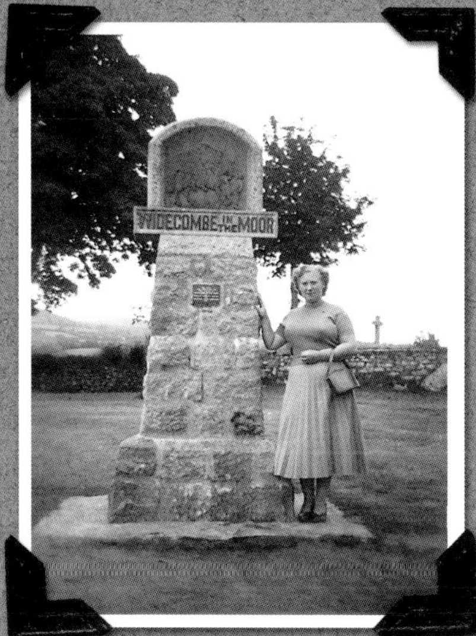

DARTMOOR

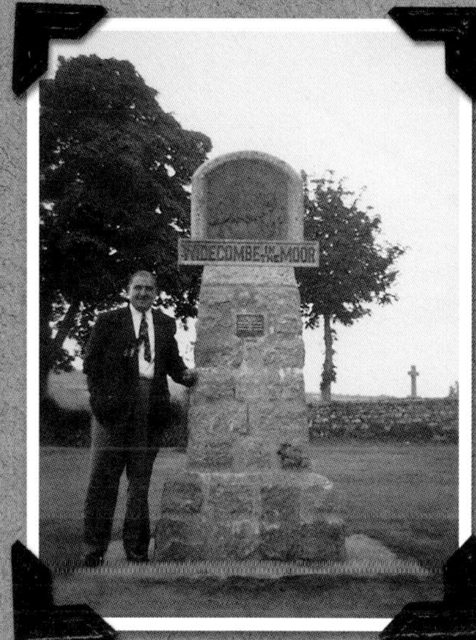

"Our holiday was finally over. We had perfect weather, plenty to eat and drink and best of all a bathe every day. Roll on next holday!"

SUNDAY 4TH SEPTEMBER

Mileage 82628 to 82798
170 miles. Petrol 4 gallons

Breakfast: Cornflakes, poached egg on toast, toast, marmalade and tea.

We left Paignton about 9 am. Not a lot of traffic on the road to start with, but it was getting thicker by the time we reached the Exeter by-pass. There was a steamer going through the canal and we were held up for about 20 minutes. After leaving Exeter we caught up with an Army convoy and it was painful for several miles. Eventually we overtook the lot and from then on it was plain sailing, eventually arriving home at Reading about 1.30 pm.

The route we had taken was as follows. Totnes, Newton Abbot, Exeter, Honiton, Ilminster, Wincanton, Amesbury, Andover and Basingstoke.

After arriving home we unpacked, had a cup of tea, then freshened ourselves up and visited the Astoria for high tea. Steak, chips, tomatoes etc, and a lager each. We then called at the Wynford for a few drinks.

Our holiday was finally over. We had had perfect weather, plenty to eat and drink and best of all, a bathe every day.

Roll on next holiday!

Newquay August 1957
(weekend short break)

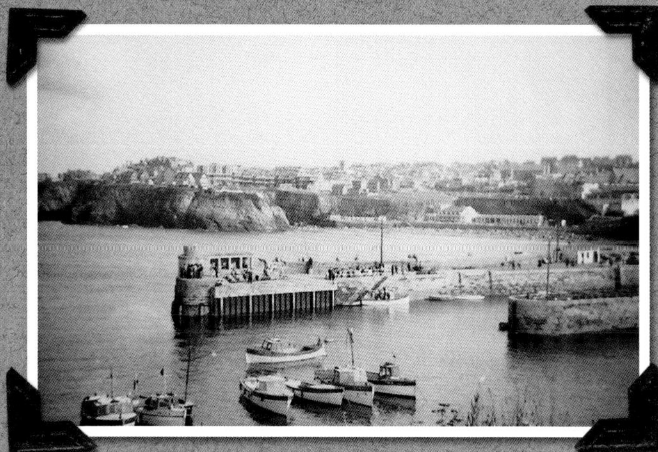

SATURDAY 5TH AUGUST

255 miles. Petrol 7 gallons

We left Reading at midnight on Friday and had quite a pleasant journey. Stopped twice for a snack and once for petrol. It rained when we reached Bodmin. We arrived at Newquay approximately 7 am, parked the car, and had a read for a while. We then had breakfast at Macaris, poached egg on toast and tea.

The rained cleared and it was a lovely sunny day, but oh so windy. We took a walk along the main street and round the harbour, then took a ride out to Fistral Beach where we took two very good photographs. We then returned to Newquay and paid a visit to the Sailor's Arms for a pint of mild and light ale, with a cornish pastie each, after which we decided we were still hungry so had lunch at Stephen's Café. Braised beef, peas, potatoes, roll and butter, rice pudding and tea. We then had a walk across the sands, after which we rode out to Crantock. We hadn't been there before and thought it a very beautiful spot, the Gannel Estuary especially so.

We then returned to Mrs Jefferies to unpack and settle in. Poor Moss was really tired and slept for about three hours. After his rest and a cup of tea he was quite refreshed and we went out about 7.30 to renew our acquaintance with the 'locals'.

We rode out to the King Mark of Cornwall, previously the Pilchard, for a port and lemon each. Then we called at the Bristol for two iced lagers and from there, to St Romans for two gin and grapefruits. Then on to the Pentire for two more iced lagers, after which we parked the car and took a walk to the Central for two John Haig scotch whiskys. Then up the hill to the Palm Court at the Atlantic for two gin and grapefruits and finished our session at the Tudor Bar with a Watneys light and a pint of Youngers.

We had a snack at the Harbour Café before turning in. Moss had two corned beef and three salmon sandwiches with two cups of tea. I had four salmon sandwiches and one cup of tea.

So home to bed after quite a hectic, but lovely day to begin our holiday.

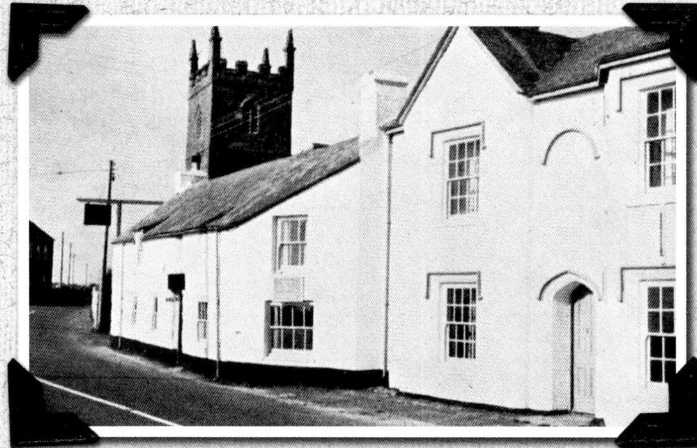

FIRST AND LAST INN, SENNEN

SUNDAY 6TH AUGUST

Mileage 143. Petrol 4 gallons

Breakfast: Cereal, egg, bacon, fried bread, toast, marmalade and tea.

We left Newquay about 9.30 am, and travelled via Redruth, Camborne and Penzance to Sennen Cove. We made a detour on the way to visit the ancient village of Carn Euny but ended up in a farmyard. Sennen Cove is a very quaint little place with a nice beach for bathing and beautiful coastal scenery. We had a drink at the Old Success Inn, pint of mild and a light ale, then took some photos before continuing on our way to Land's End.

Although a magnificent piece of coastal scenery, it is marred with refuse lying around. Anyway, we had a stroll around and partook of two Whitbread light ales at the Last Hotel, before carrying on to Logan's Rock, a beauty spot we missed last holiday. We parked the car at Treen and walked about a half a mile to reach the rock. Here again the cliffs were magnificent and the beaches at Porthcurno, which can be seen from Logan's Rock, looked lovely.

The weather today has been grand and though still quite windy, the sun is really warm. We made our way to St Ives via St Just and had a late lunch at the Harbour Café. Rump steak, onions, chips, bread, butter and tea. We didn't stay long at St Ives as we wish to spend a whole day here later, so we rode back to Newquay via Hayle etc.

In the evening we took a ride out to Perranporth and had a drink at the hotel of that name. We had two Whitbread lights and then two more light ales at the Tywarnhayle Hotel, where we tried to play the local game. Then back to Newquay via Cubert and Holywell Bay. We stopped at the Hotel Bristol for two iced lagers, and the Great Western for two gin and grapefruits. Then up to the Atlantic Palm Court for two Harveys Bristol dry sherries, where we heard a beautiful piece of piano playing by a blind young man. We then went down to the Tudor Bar to partake of a pint and a half of Youngers, after which we parked the car and took a walk to the Sailor's Arms, where we finished our evening with a light ale and mild and light ale, together with steak and kidney pies.

It had rained heavily but cleared long enough for us to walk home in the dry.

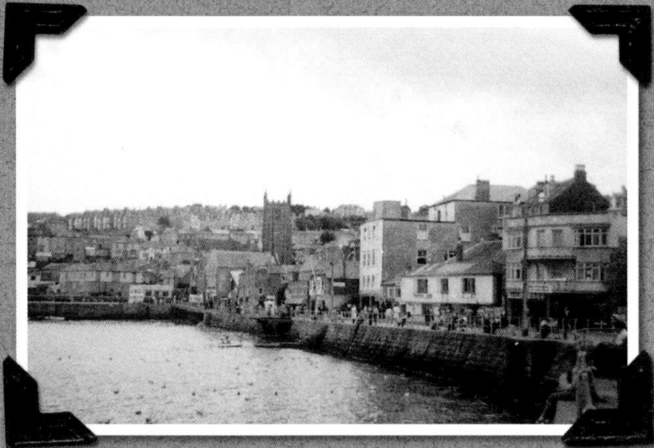

ST IVES

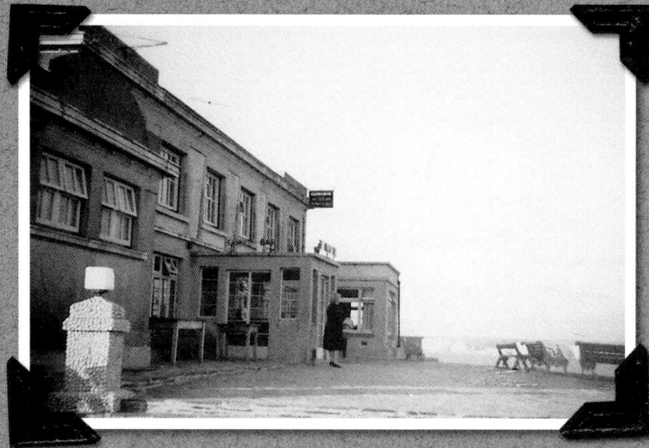

TUDOR BAR, NEWQUAY

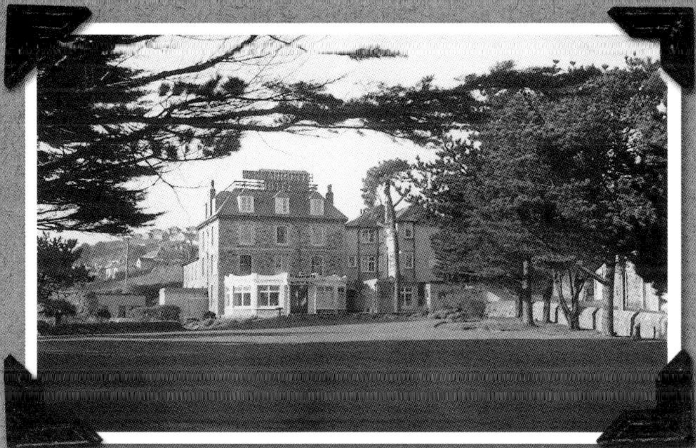

PERRANPORTH HOTEL

"We then returned to Newquay and paid a visit to the Sailor's Arms for a pint of mild and light ale, with a cornish pastie each, after which we decided we were still hungry so had lunch at Stephen's Café. Braised beef, peas, potatoes, roll and butter, rice pudding and tea."

Monday 7th August

Mileage 136. Petrol 3 gallons

Breakfast: Grapefruit, spam, fried bread, tomatoes, toast, marmalade and tea.

We intended visiting Plymouth today, but after only going a couple of miles the car gave us some trouble so we had to return to Newquay where, at the Tower Garage, they put it right by installing a new petrol flex. Whilst this was being attended to we called at the Harbour Café for a cup of tea and corned beef sandwiches. Eventually at about 11.30 we started out for Truro and had a look at the shops and also the cathedral.

Then on to St Austell for another walk round and a light ale and mild and light ale. The weather is still very good and although it rained early this morning, the sun is now shining. We then returned to Newquay and had a meal at the Coffee Pot. Bacon, sausage, egg, tomato, chips, bread, butter and tea. Then we washed and changed early as we wanted to take a ride out to Bolventor to visit the Jamaica Inn. It was an extremely pleasant ride and a beautiful Summer's evening. After having a drink, pint of bitter and light ale, we made our way back to Newquay, calling at the Garland Ox, Bodmin, for a light ale and a light and mild.

On the road back we saw a sign post which looked promising, advertising the Royal Oak, Blisland, so thought we would investigate. It did not live up to expectations. Still, we had a drink, Whitbread light and a light and mild. Then on to the Victoria at Roche, which proved to be an extremely worthwhile stop. The place itself is extremely quaint

"Then we washed and changed early as we wanted to take a ride out to Bolventor to visit the Jamaica Inn. It was an extremely pleasant ride and a beautiful Summer's evening."

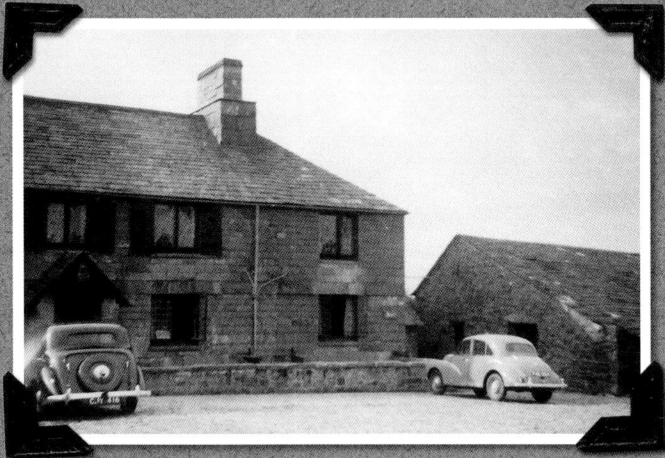

JAMAICA INN

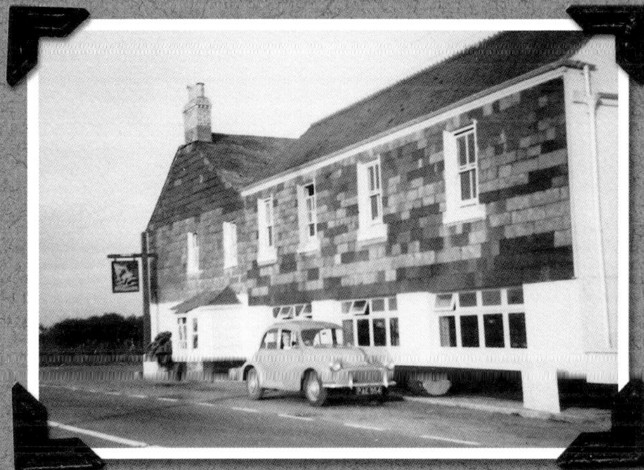

VICTORIA INN, ROCHE

and the food they serve is delicious. We had a dry sherry and a lager each to help down two rounds of beef sandwiches, after which we decided we would return there another day to sample a grill.

We then continued on our way to the King Mark for two port and lemons and the Tudor Bar for a pint and a half of Youngers, after which we parked the car. We took a walk to the New Inn for two Whitbread lights and the Central for two gin and grapefruits. We then had 6d of chips each and called at the Harbour Café for a cup of tea and salmon sandwiches.

So ended our lovely weekend break. The weather has been beautiful and we look forward to our next visit.

Newquay August 1958

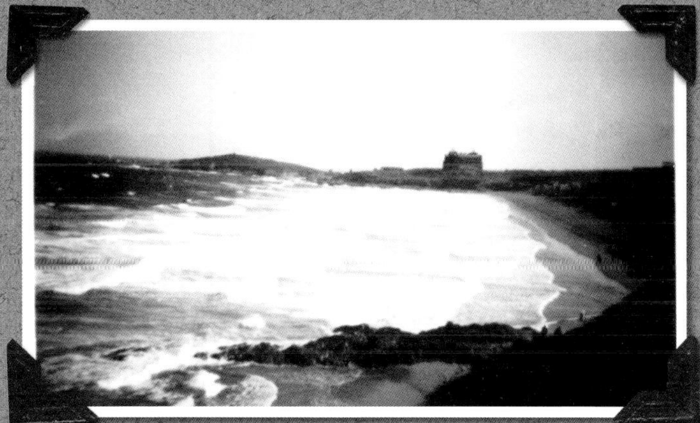

SATURDAY 16TH AUGUST

Mileage 14400 to 144261
261 miles. Petrol 9 gallons

We left Reading at 1.30 am and arrived in Newquay about 8am. It was a lovely night, though quite a bit of traffic on the road. We had two stops for tea and cake. On arriving at Newquay we parked behind the Atlantic Hotel, overlooking the headland, and finished up our eats. We then slept for an hour or so. About 10 o'clock we decided to visit Mrs Jefferies and see if it was a convenient time to unpack etc, but on arriving there, we found that Mrs Jefferies had not booked us a room. Fortunately we were able to get fixed up next door with the Misses Jackson, which was a good stroke of luck.

After unpacking and having a wash and change, we took a walk through the shopping centre of Newquay to the Bristol Hotel where Maurice had two lagers and I had one. We then strolled back to the Coffee Pot where we had lunch. Soup followed by sausage, bacon, egg, chips, bread and butter. In the afternoon we walked out to the headland, a thing we had not done on previous visits.

I was a beautiful day and of course, we were hoping the weather was going to stay that way. We had our tea at the Harbour Café, cups of tea with salmon sandwiches.

In the evening we went to Perranporth, the Tywarnhayle Hotel, for a pint of best for Maury, and a light ale for myself. We then called at the Perranporth Hotel for a half pint of best (M) and a tomato juice (B). We then rode back to Crantock to the Old Albion where Maury

“We left Reading at 1.30 am and arrived in Newquay about 8am...but on arriving there, we found that Mrs Jefferies had not booked us a room.”

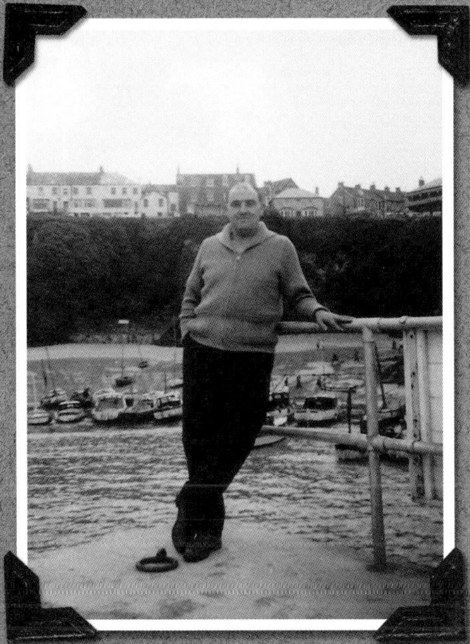

NEWQUAY HARBOUR

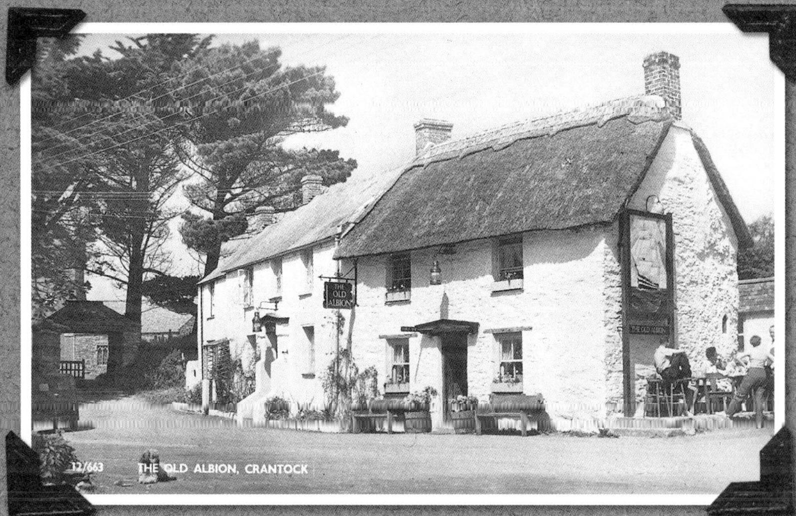

OLD ALBION, CRANTOCK

had two lagers and I had one. This is rather a quaint little Inn, very old. We then carried on back to Newquay.

Next to the King Mark for two light ales, and then to the Tudor Bar where Maury had two pints of Watneys, and I had two bitter lemons. We were getting hungry again by this time, so we parked the car and took a walk to the Sailor's Arms, where Maury had a pint of best and I had a light ale, plus a steak and kidney pie each. Very tasty!

We finished our first evening at the Harbour Café with tea and ham sandwiches.

SUNDAY 17TH AUGUST

Mileage 144261 to 144372
109 miles (Beryl 42, Maurice 67). Petrol 3 gallons

Our first night in twin beds! Had a good night's sleep, no doubt we must have been very tired. Early morning tea, then breakfast at 9 o'clock. Grapefruit, bacon, egg, fried bread, tomato, bread and butter, toast and marmalade and tea. A very good breakfast, nicely cooked.

Our objective today was the Lizard and we went via Helston, where we had a short walk around. The weather was still OK. On arriving at the Lizard we parked the car, and then walked across the fields to Lizard Point, had a short sit down, then continued round the cliff to the light house. We called at Wave Crest Café and had a grapefruit each, ordered lunch, and sat outside in the beautiful sunshine. We had lunch outside as it was so nice;

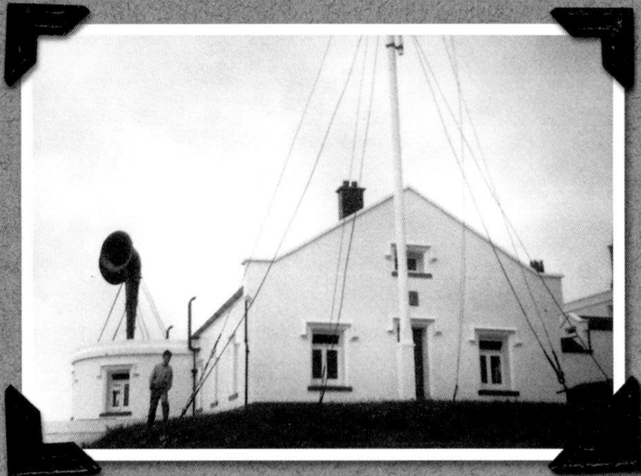

"Our first night in twin beds. Had a good night's sleep, no doubt we must have been very tired."

LIZARD POINT

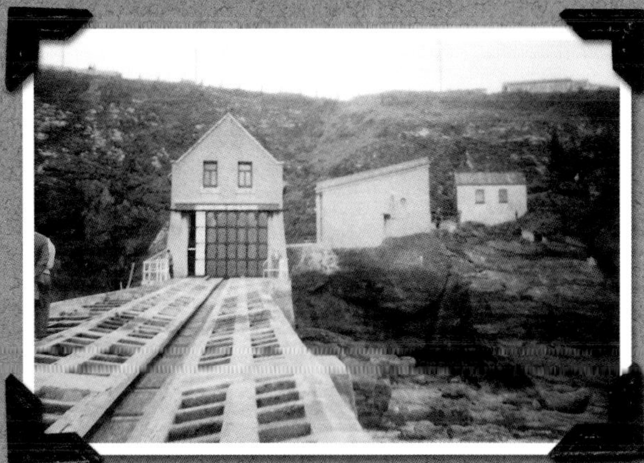

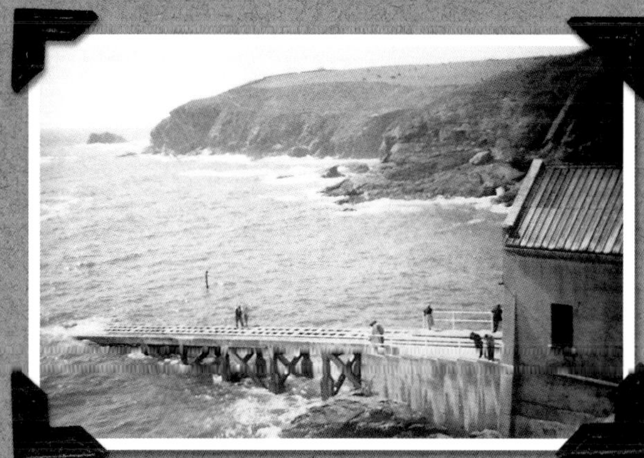

roast beef, boiled potatoes and cabbage, bread and butter, fruit salad with cream, and tea.

After this we visited Kynance Cove, a very beautiful spot. We actually walked down to the beach, what a climb back up though! We sat in the sun for an hour or so on the cliff top, then made our way back to Newquay to wash and change, ready for the evening.

Our first call was the Victoria at Roche where we partook of two lagers each with three rounds of tongue and two rounds of chicken sandwiches. Very tasty. Back to Newquay to call at the Bristol for a lager each, St Romans for a sherry each, Tudor bar for a pint of Watneys Red Barrel and a light ale, and finished up at the Central Hotel with another sherry each.

MONDAY 18TH AUGUST

Mileage 144372 to 144522
150 miles (Beryl 50). Petrol 4 gallons

Early morning tea, then breakfast. Cornflakes, bacon, fried bread, egg, bread and butter, toast and marmalade and tea.

Our destination this morning was Plymouth, and we decided to go via Tor Point Ferry, a mistake on our part as we had a two hour wait. We passed the time by eating pears and I did some knitting. On reaching Plymouth at 1.30 we straight away had lunch at Spooner's Capri Restaurant. Maury had roast beef, potatoes, peas, rice pudding and orangeade. I had roast pork, stuffing, potatoes, peas, rice pudding and grapefruit juice.

After lunch we had a walk around the shops and bought our holiday diary and Bambi. It wasn't quite such good weather, one or two showers, but nothing to grumble about. We returned to Newquay via Tavistock, a very pretty ride across the edge of Dartmoor. We called at the Harbour Café for tea, two rounds of salmon sandwiches, four eccles cakes and tea. We then washed and changed ready for the evening.

Our first objective was the Pheasant Inn at Newlyn East, which wasn't up to our expectations. Maurice had a pint of Bass and I, a light ale. Then the London Inn for a pint of best (M) and a light ale (B), the Blue Anchor for half a pint of best and a tomato juice and the Kings Head for half a pint of best and a light ale. Then back to the Pentire at Newquay for a pint of Watneys and a light ale for Maurice and a bitter lemon for myself. We then went to the Sailor's Arms for a snack, two steak and kidney pies, which Maury washed down with a pint of best, and I had a light ale.

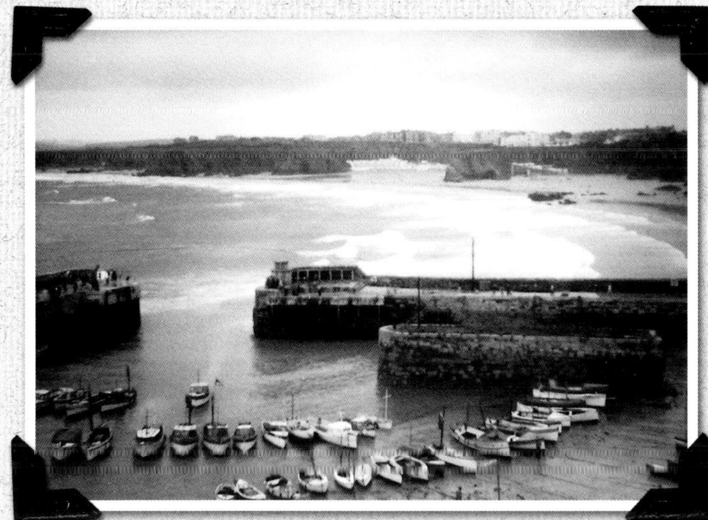

Our last call was the Harbour Café for the inevitable cup of tea for myself, coffee for Maury and salmon sandwiches each.

Tuesday 19th August

Mileage 144552 to 144654
102 miles (Beryl 48 and Maurice 54). Petrol 4 gallons

Early morning cuppa, then breakfast. Porridge, sausage, bacon, fried bread, tomato, bread and butter, toast and marmalade and tea.

We took the coast road North, going through Porth, Watergate Bay etc, to Trevose Head. Had a walk out to the headland, very beautiful coastal scenery, then carried on to Padstow. It started to rain so we called at the London Inn, a nice little pub, where Maury had a pint of draft and myself, a light ale. We then continued on to Boscastle, where we ran into a heavy storm. Took refuge in the Napoleon Inn, a very quaint place, where we had a lager each, and ordered lunch. Infra red steak, chips, bread and butter. Delish! Owing to the storm the electric was cut, but luckily our lunch was just ready. We had another lager each, then thought it best to make our way back to Newquay, via Wadebridge.

It was fine when we arrived back so had a walk around the shops, then had tea at the Harbour Café, H & P's fruit cake and tea. We then washed and changed ready for the evening.

Decided to visit some pubs around Truro, making our first call the Red Lion in the centre of Truro. Quite a nice bar. We had a lager each then took the Falmouth road to call at the Norway Inn, one of the best places for a drink we visited this year. Maurice had a pint of best draft and I had a light ale. Then we managed to find the Punch Bowl and Ladle at Feock, but this place was rather disappointing. I had a bitter lemon and Maury, half a pint of Flowers best draft.

"...then took the Falmouth road to call at the Norway Inn, one of the best places for a drink we visited this year."

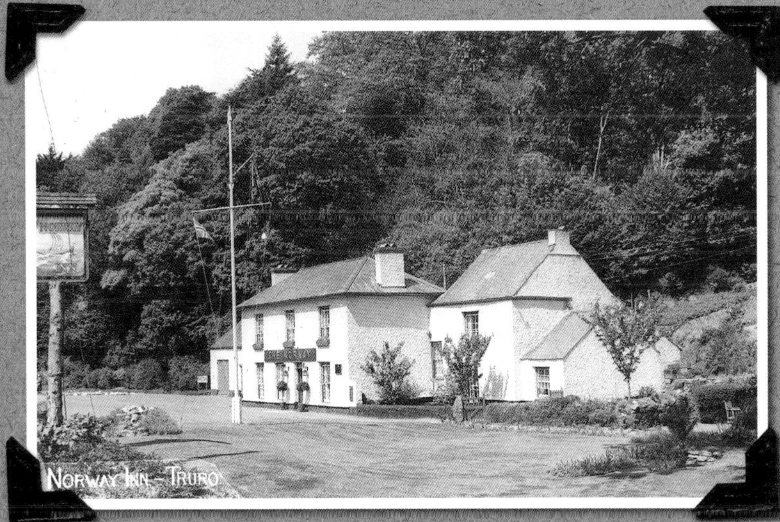

NORWAY INN, PERRAN-AR-WORTHAL

We then made our way back to Truro and took the Bodmin road, calling at the Wheel Inn, Tresillian for a light ale and half of draft best. The storm earlier in the day had been pretty bad around here and several houses, including the Wheel Inn, had been flooded. We saw lino and carpets hanging out to dry.

Back to Newquay, Tudor Bar, for a pint of Watneys and a light ale. Then the Sailor's Arms for our supper snack, steak and kidney pie each with a pint of draft bass and a light ale. Last call, the Harbour Café for a cuppa.

Wednesday 20th August

Mileage 144654 to 144800
146 miles (Beryl 33). Petrol 4 gallons

Early morning tea, then breakfast. Grapefruit, bacon, fried bread, egg, bread and butter, toast and marmalade and tea.

It was a fine morning. Destination Penzance via Redruth, Camborne, Hayle. It was raining when we reached Penzance, so we carried on to Newlyn, Mousehole and Porthcurno. Fine here, so had a walk down to the beach. Nowhere to have a snack so decided to make for Sennen Cove. Had a drink at the Old Success Inn, a pint of best bitter for Maurice and I had a light ale.

It came on to rain very hard so we had our lunch at the Cove Café. We both had roast beef, potatoes, carrots, peas, followed by apple and custard for Maurice and jam tart and custard for Beryl. The rain had settled down to a heavy drizzle so we returned to Newquay via

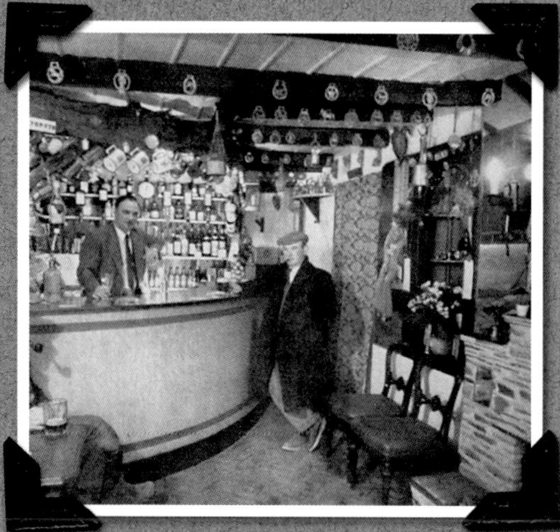

MINERS ARMS, MITHIAN

"The storm earlier in the day had been pretty bad around here and several houses, including the Wheel Inn, had been flooded. We saw lino and carpets hanging out to dry."

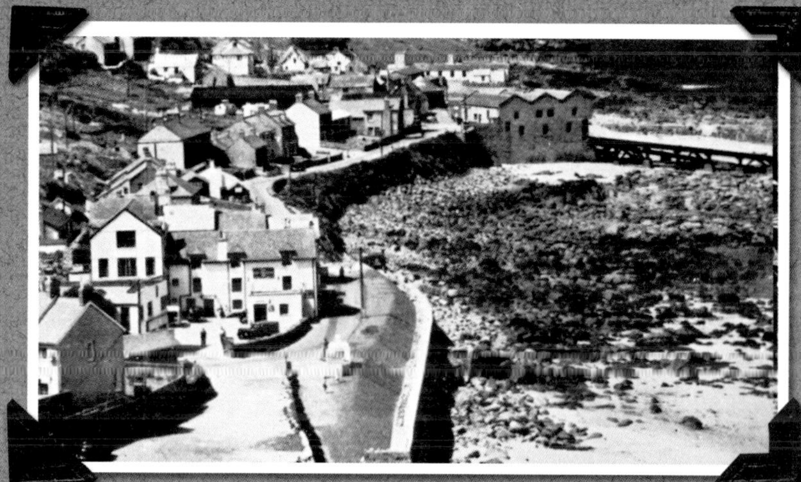

OLD SUCCESS INN, SENNEN COVE

Penzance and Redruth. On reaching Newquay we called at the Harbour Café for tea. Salmon sandwiches and fruit cake for Maurice, buttered scone and fruit cake for me.

We returned to our digs to wash and change for the evening, which wasn't very pleasant as regards the weather. We followed a guide book and called at the following places. Fox and Hounds at Scorrier nr Redruth. Maurice had a pint of draft best and I had a light ale. Not a bad little pub. Victoria Inn at Three Mile Stone. We had a bitter lemon each. This was not in the guide book but it was quite a nice little place. Plume of Feathers at Scorrier. Maurice had half of draft best and I had a light ale. This is a very nice place. Chiverton Arms, Blackwater. Maury had a pint of draft best and I, a tomato juice. We also partook of two steak pies. This also was a pleasant little pub.

The Railway Inn at St Agnes. Maurice had a half of draft bitter and Beryl a light ale. Driftwood Spars, Trevaunance Cove, St Agnes.

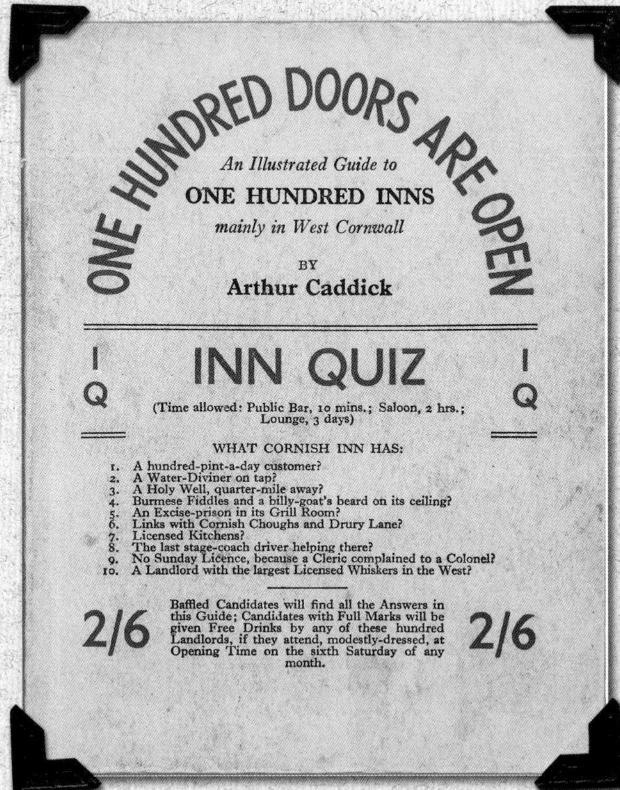
ONE HUNDRED DOORS ARE OPEN

An Illustrated Guide to

ONE HUNDRED INNS

mainly in West Cornwall

BY

Arthur Caddick

I Q — INN QUIZ — I Q

(Time allowed: Public Bar, 10 mins.; Saloon, 2 hrs.; Lounge, 3 days)

WHAT CORNISH INN HAS:

1. A hundred-pint-a-day customer?
2. A Water-Diviner on tap?
3. A Holy Well, quarter-mile away?
4. Burmese Fiddles and a billy-goat's beard on its ceiling?
5. An Excise-prison in its Grill Room?
6. Links with Cornish Choughs and Drury Lane?
7. Licensed Kitchens?
8. The last stage-coach driver helping there?
9. No Sunday Licence, because a Cleric complained to a Colonel?
10. A Landlord with the largest Licensed Whiskers in the West?

2/6 — Baffled Candidates will find all the Answers in this Guide; Candidates with Full Marks will be given Free Drinks by any of these hundred Landlords, if they attend, modestly-dressed, at Opening Time on the sixth Saturday of any month. — 2/6

"We followed a guide book and called at the following places..."

I had a bitter lemon and Maurice a gin and grapefruit. This place is not at all up to standard, rather dirty and nothing unique about it. Miners Arms, Mithian. Maurice half of draft best. Beryl a light ale. Rather a small bar, but very quaint. The sort of place one expects to find in the country. Quintrell Inn. Maurice had half of draft best and I had a light ale. Very bare place, not worth a second visit. Finally, The King Mark for a Babycham each.

Then back to the Harbour Café for tea and salmon sandwiches (M) and egg, tomato sandwiches (B)

Thursday 21st August

Mileage 144800 to 144908
108 miles (Beryl 60). Petrol 4 gallons

Early morning tea, then breakfast. Prunes, bacon, fried spam, fried bread, tomatoes, bread and butter, toast and marmalade and tea.

Our destination was Looe, via Bodmin and Liskeard. We stopped at the Punch Bowl Inn at Lanreath, a very nice place indeed, and partook of a lager each. We then carried on to Looe for lunch at the Golden Guinea. Tomato soup with a bread roll each, lamb chop, potatoes, carrots and peas (Beryl) and liver, sausage and chips (Maurice), gooseberry pie each with tea. A very nice meal, after which we took a walk through Looe and sat for a while on Banjo pier.

As it was nice and sunny we carried on to Polperro, looked at the model village, not up to much, then sat out on the rocks for an hour or so sunning ourselves. Our return journey was via Liskeard, and we then stopped at the Jamaica Inn, Bolventor, for a light ale (B) and two ciders (M). We also stopped at the Lanivet Inn for a pint of St Austell Extra (M) and a bitter lemon (B). Also the Victoria Inn at Roche for two lagers and a round of tongue sandwiches each.

Then back to Newquay to wash and change. We took a walk, calling at the New Inn for a tomato juice and half best draft, and the Victoria for a light ale and half draft bitter. It started to rain so we made our way back to the Tudor Bar. Three pints of Watneys and a Dimple scotch (M), and one Watneys light ale, two bitter lemons and a Dimple scotch (B).

By now it was raining very heavy and had to make a run for our digs.

FRIDAY 22ND AUGUST

Mileage 144908 to 145039
131 miles (Beryl 60). Petrol 4 gallons

Early morning tea, then breakfast. Grapefruit, bacon, fried bread, egg, bread and butter, toast and marmalade and tea.

Very wet morning. Went to Mevagissey, parked on the harbour and had tea and choc rolls at a café. Rain cleared up a little and we were able to walk around, then toured the coast to St Mawes. Back to Newquay for salmon sandwiches, cake and tea at the Harbour Café. Then washed and changed for the evening.

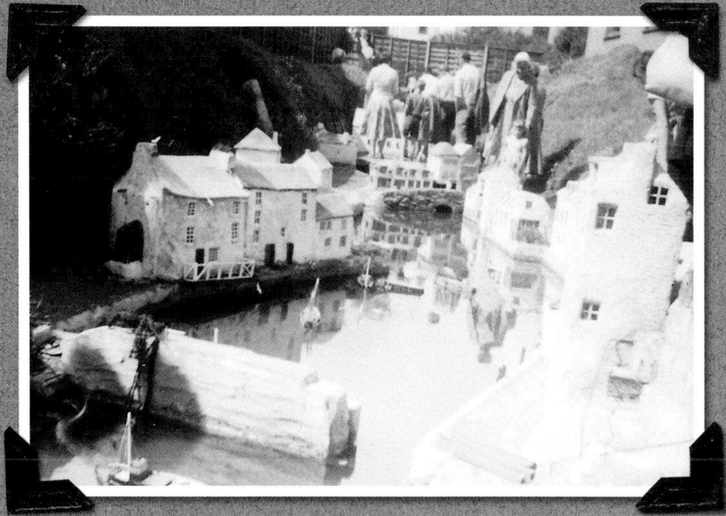

POLPERRO MODEL VILLAGE

"As it was nice and sunny
we carried on to Polperro,
looked at the model village"

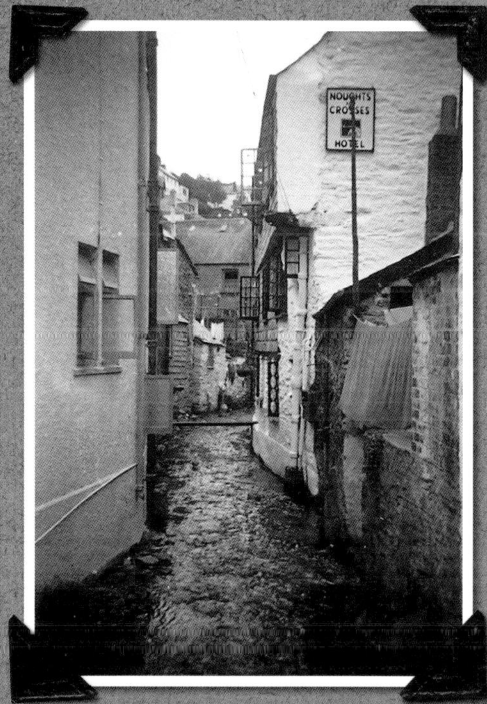

POLPERRO

Rode out to Bodmin, Cat and Fiddle, for a light ale and a pint of best draft. Then to the Victoria at Roche for two lagers each and two Bristol Milk sherries. For dinner we both had soup, rump steak, chips, peas and runner beans followed by bananas and cream. Delish!

Back to the Tudor Bar at Newquay for a pint of Watneys (Maury) and a Watneys light ale (Beryl). Finished up at the Harbour Café for two teas.

Saturday 23rd August

Mileage 145039 to 145182
143 miles (Beryl 67). Petrol 4 gallons

Early morning tea, then breakfast. Porridge, bacon, scrambled eggs, fried bread, tomatoes, bread and butter, toast and marmalade and tea.

A lovely day. Went to Portreath and sat on the wall in the sunshine. Took photos, then on to Hayle via Hells Mouth, then to St Ives. For lunch we had steak pie, chips, peas, bread and butter and tea. Then walked round for a while before carrying on to Cape Cornwall, a very pleasant spot. We climbed to the top, then had an ice cream to cool off before carrying on to Land's End.

We returned to Newquay via Penzance, Hayle and Redruth etc. It rained a little. Called at the Harbour Café for our tea, cheese and tomato and salmon sandwiches, cake and tea. Took an evening trip to the Molesworthy Arms at Wadebridge for a pint of best draft (M) and a light ale (B). Then to the Swan Hotel for a bitter lemon and half a best bitter, Ring of Bells at

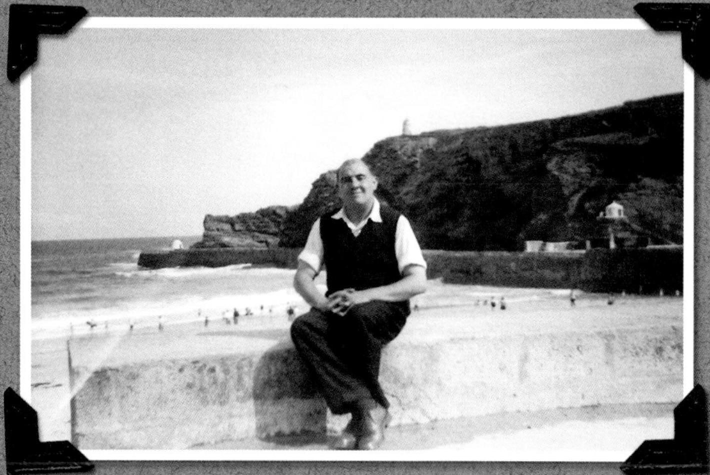

"Went to Portreath and sat on the wall in the sunshine."

PORTREATH

ST IVES

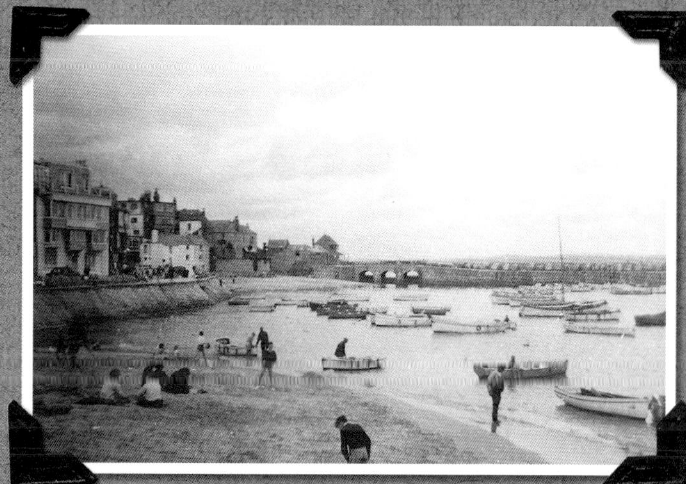

St Issey for a light ale and pint of best draft, King Mark for a bitter lemon and half of draft, Sailor's Arms for a light ale and a pint of bitter, plus a cornish pastie each, and finally the Tudor Bar for a pint of Watneys and a light ale.

Supper at the Harbour Café. Two teas each with egg and tomato plus cheese and tomato sandwiches (M), egg and tomato sandwiches and fruit cake (B).

Sunday 24th August

Mileage 145182 to 145445
263 miles (Beryl 90). Petrol 6 gallons

Early morning tea then breakfast. Cornflakes, bacon, egg, fried bread, tomato, bread and butter, toast and marmalade and tea.

A very wet morning. Decided to take a trip across to Bow Bridge and look up 'Dear Boy'. Went via Tor Point ferry as it was too bad to go across Dartmoor. Luckily, we caught the first ferry. We were disappointed on reaching the Watermans as 'Dear Boy' had left. Anyway, we had a snack of bread, cheese and pickled onions. Maury had a pint of draft and I had a light ale.

We then carried on to Paignton and called at the Waterside for two light ales. Rode onto Torquay, which was deserted owing to the bad weather. Returned via Plymouth, where we stopped for tea and cakes, Tavistock, Liskeard, Bodmin and to Newquay, by which time the weather had cleared up a little, with spells of sunshine.

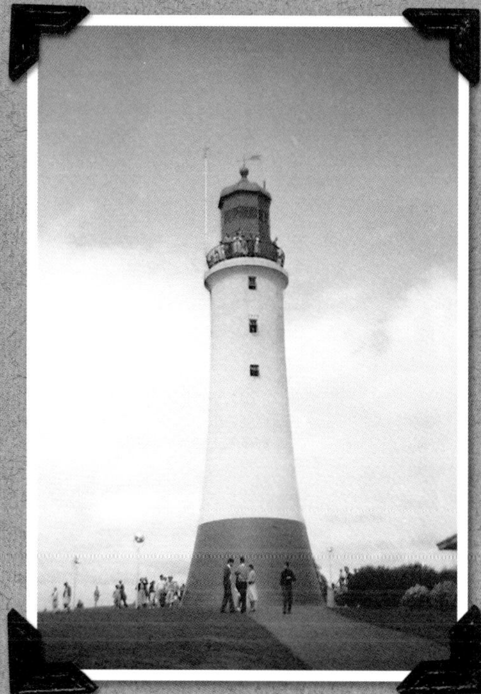

PLYMOUTH

"So finished an unpleasant day, as far as the weather was concerned."

In the evening we sorted some more inns out of the guide. The Lamb and Flag, for a light ale and a pint of draft, Goughs Inn, Camborne, for a pint of draft and a light ale, and two rounds of brisket of beef sandwiches. The Chiverton Arms, for a pint and a light ale, Hawkins Arms, Zelah, for a light ale and half a pint. St Romans for a light ale and half a draft, the Red Lion for a light ale and half a draft.

So finished an unpleasant day, as far as the weather was concerned.

MONDAY 25TH AUGUST

Mileage 145445 to 145539
94 miles (Beryl 56). Petrol 3 gallons

Early morning tea, then breakfast. Porridge, bacon, egg, fried bead, tomato, bread and butter, toast and marmalade and tea.

A lovely day. Went to Fowey and had a walk round, and a cup of tea in a cosy caf . Then we took a river trip, very nice indeed. Had lunch at Fowey, steak pie, potatoes, carrots, peas, followed by apricots and custard.

We then travelled on via Carlyon Bay, a very pretty spot, Charlestown, we spent a while on the harbour, and Mevagissey, where we sat on the harbour wall enjoying the lovely sunshine. We then returned to Newquay.

Evening destination; The Victoria at Roche for dinner. Appetisers; Beryl one lager, Maury two

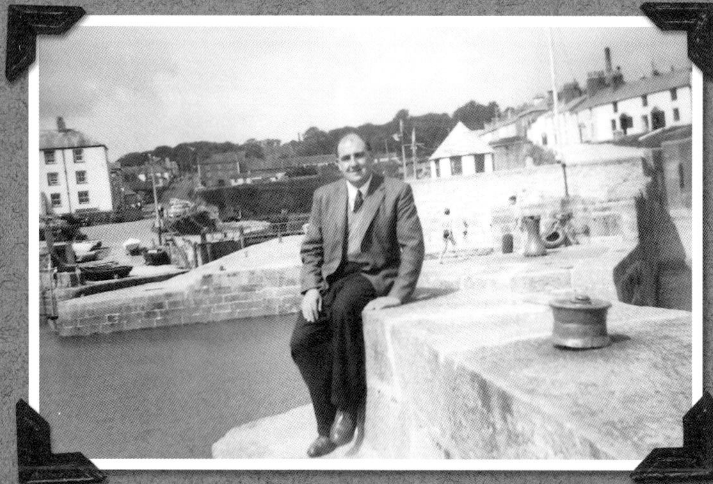

CHARLESTOWN

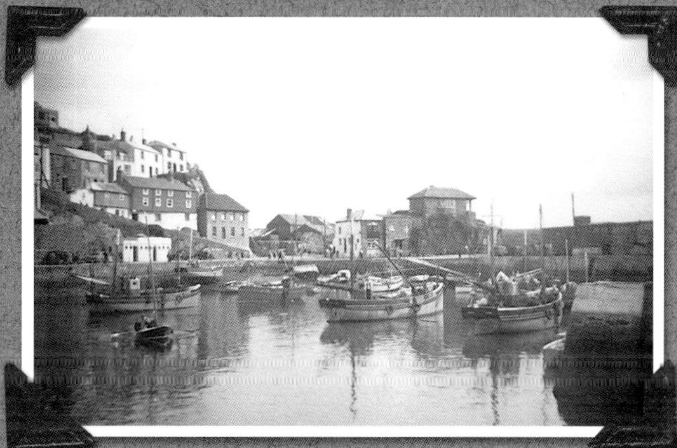

MEVAGISSEY

"We then travelled on via Carlyon Bay, a very pretty spot, Charlestown, we spent a while on the harbour, and Mevagissey, where we sat on the harbour wall enjoying the lovely sunshine."

pints of St Austell Extra. Then a Madeira sherry and a Bristol Milk sherry each. Dinner: Soup, steak, chips, peas, runner beans, followed by fruit sundae.

We returned to Newquay and had a walk, finally calling at the Harbour Café for tea and sandwiches.

TUESDAY 26TH AUGUST

Mileage 145539 to 145719
180 miles (Beryl 52). Petrol 4 gallons

Early morning tea, then breakfast: Grapefruit, bacon, sausage, fried bread, tomato, bread and butter, toast and marmalade and tea.

Rather dull and overcast this morning. Anyway, we set out for the Lizard, one of our favourite spots. Had a walk round the lighthouse point and by the life boat house, and called at the Wave Crest Café for a lemon and orangeade. Carried on after this to Mullion, a quaint little harbour, and visited the Old Inn for a light ale and half a draft.

Onto Poldhu Cove, a pleasant spot. Across country to Coverack, calling at the Wheel Inn for a light ale and half a draft, and two rounds of cheese and tomato sandwiches each. Quite a nice little pub. Onto Gweek, Helford Bridge and Falmouth. Ran into rain, but parked the car and took a walk. Then to Penryn, Truro and back to Newquay, where we visited the Harbour Café for two teas each with salmon sandwiches and cake.

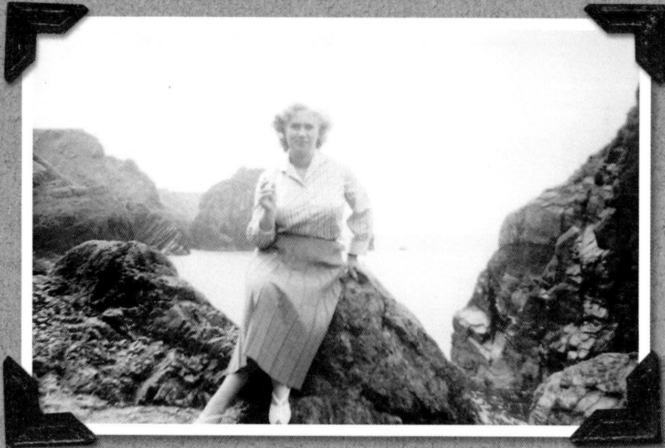

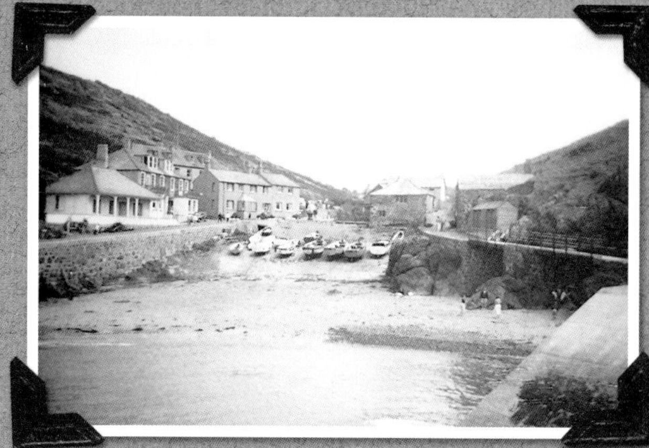

MULLION

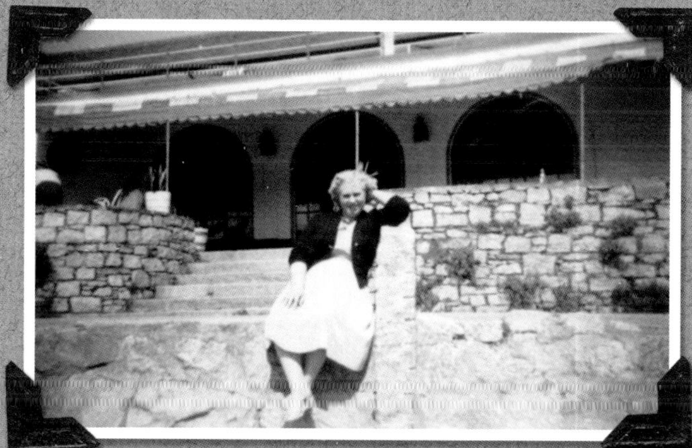

FERRYBOAT INN, HELFORD, NEAR GWEEK

Had a little tour in the evening. First call, the Plume of Feathers at Penhallow, for a pint of best and a Worthington. London Hotel, Redruth, for a half of draft and a bitter lemon. Plough Inn, Camborne, for a light ale and half a draft. Smugglers Inn, St Erth, for a pint of Watneys and a light ale. This is the Inn we failed to find earlier on. Halfway House, for a tomato juice, half a draft and cheese biscuits. Duke of Leeds, Leedstown, bitter lemon and half a draft.

We returned to Hayle and bought some chips, which went down well. Next to the Angarrack Inn, Angarrack, for a light ale and half a draft best. What a dump. Should never be in the book. Back to Newquay for cheese and tomato sandwiches, cake and tea, at the Harbour Café.

Wednesday 27th August

Mileage 145719 to 145900
181 miles (Beryl 74). Petrol 5 gallons

Early morning tea. Breakfast: Cornflakes, bacon, fried bread, egg, bread and butter, toast and marmalade and tea.

Our destination, Clovelly. Stopped at Bude on the way for a walk around the shops. Had a snack, a cup of tea and a swiss roll. Quite a nice day. Strolled through Clovelly to the harbour, and called at the Red Lion for a light ale and half a draft best. Then had lunch there. Mushroom soup, roast beef, yorkshire pudding, peas, potatoes, followed by gooseberry pie. Then made our way back to the car park. What a climb, but not quite so puffed as previous years though.

On the journey back to Newquay we ran into rain. We visited the Harbour Café for a cuppa and salmon sandwiches.

In the evening we went to the Victoria Inn at Roche. Maurice had three pints of St Austell Extra and I had two lagers. Dinner: Chicken salad, bread and butter, and topped up with a Tia Maria (B) and a Drambuie (M). Carried on to the Fox and Hounds for half a draft best and a bitter lemon. Then to the Chiverton Arms for half a draft best and a light ale. Last pub call was the Tudor Bar. Maurice, three pints of Watneys and Beryl, two Watneys Lights.

Supper at the Harbour Café , tea and salmon sandwiches.

Thursday 28th August

Mileage 145900 and 146028
128 miles (Beryl 48). Petrol 4 gallons

Early morning tea. Breakfast: Prunes, bacon, fried bread, scrambled eggs, tomato, bread and butter, toast and marmalade and tea.

Very dull morning with rain. Decided to tour the South Cornwall coast, and our journey took us through Truro, Helston, Praa sands, where we had a walk, Marazion, had a walk to St Michael's Mount, and on to Penzance.

We called at the Pirate Inn, a nice Simonds pub, where M had a pint and half of 'heavy' with cheese and tomato sandwiches, and B had one 'SB' with fresh crab sandwiches. Very tasty!

Had a walk round Penzance shopping centre, and back to Newquay via Hayle, Camborne etc. Called at the Harbour Café for tea and salmon sandwiches. Then had a walk through Newquay, after which we returned to our digs to start packing ready for going home.

In the evening we ran out to Bodmin and called at the Lanivet Inn for half a draft best and a light ale. Then on to the Victoria at Roche for two pints of St Austell Extra and two lagers, plus a Dry Sack sherry each. For dinner, we had soup, rump steak, chips, peas, runner beans, then fruit sundae and an apricot brandy each.

Back to Newquay to the Tudor bar for a pint of Watneys and half a Red Barrel. Finally, to the Harbour Café for two teas.

FRIDAY AUGUST 29TH

Mileage 146028 to 146297
269 miles (Beryl 110). Petrol 7 gallons

Early morning tea. Breakfast: Porridge, bacon, fried bread, egg, bread and butter, toast and marmalade and tea.

We decided to return home today via the North coast road. It was a lovely morning, and we left Newquay at 9.40.

Our first stop was Ilfracombe where we had lunch. (M) steak, tomatoes, chips.
(B) plaice and chips. Bread and butter and tea each. We did a little shopping, then carried on

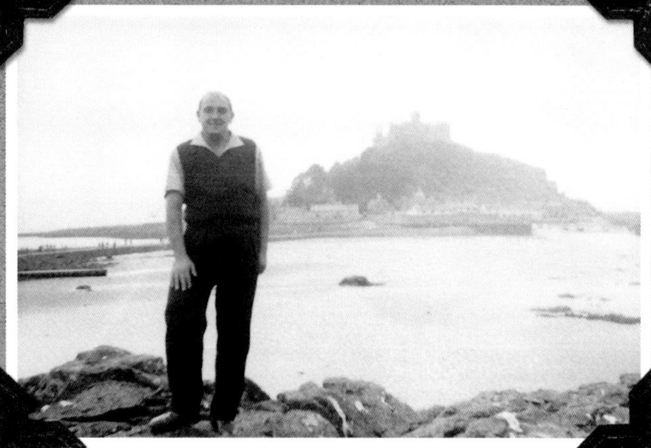

St Michael's Mount

"The weather could have been better, but after all, a holiday is what you make it."

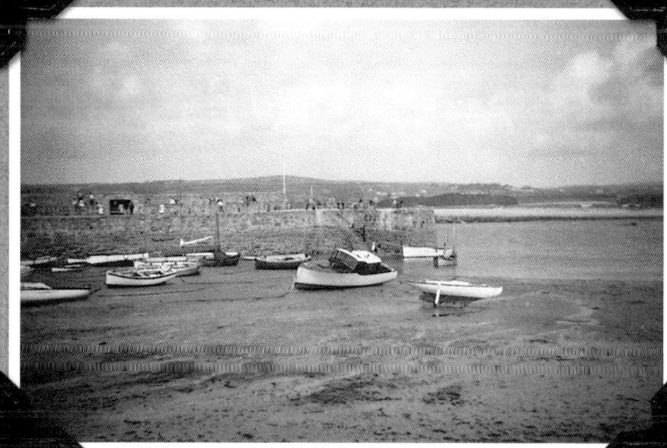

St Michael's Mount Harbour

to Lynmouth, where we had another walk round and partook of tea and cake.

Our journey took us on via Bridgewater, Glastonbury, Shepton Mallet, Frome and Trowbridge. We stopped at the George for a pint of best and a light ale, with ham sandwiches. Then carried on to the Coach and Horses at Beckhampton, for a pint of best and a light ale, together with bread, cheese and pickled onions. Then to the Hare and Hounds at Speen for two lagers, and the 'old faithful', the Travellers at Calcot, for two pints of Worthington (M) and a lager (B).

Arrived home at 9 o'clock, unpacked, then had supper. Grilled gammon and tomatoes, bread, butter and tea.

A perfect day for the journey home.

Saturday and Sunday

The weather was lovely, and we decided to take it easy.

Maury tidied up the garden while I did the washing and cleaned the place up. The rest of the time, we just lazed. Had a run out to the Palmers Arms to see Bert and Mrs Brind.

Speaking generally, we had a good holiday with plenty of nice eats and drinks. The weather could have been better, but after all, a holiday is what you make it.

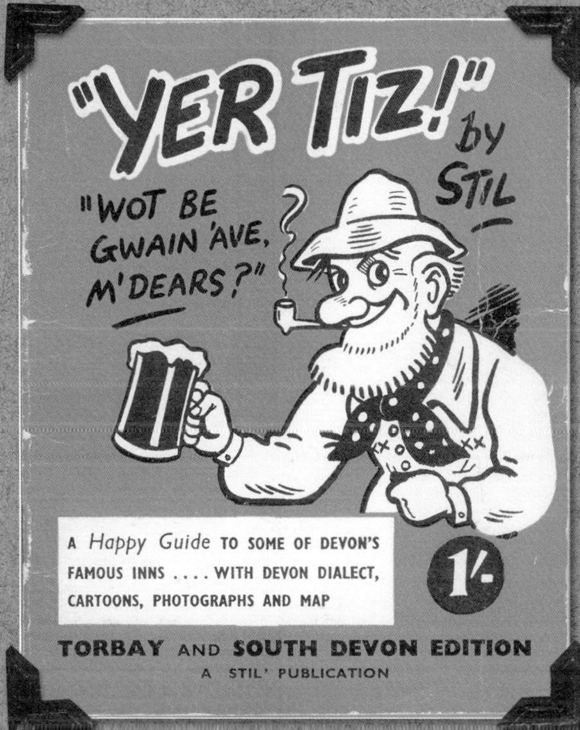
"YER TIZ!" by STIL
"WOT BE GWAIN 'AVE, M'DEARS?"
A Happy Guide TO SOME OF DEVON'S FAMOUS INNS . . . . WITH DEVON DIALECT, CARTOONS, PHOTOGRAPHS AND MAP
1/-
TORBAY AND SOUTH DEVON EDITION
A STIL' PUBLICATION

3/6

Recommended

Wayside Inns of England

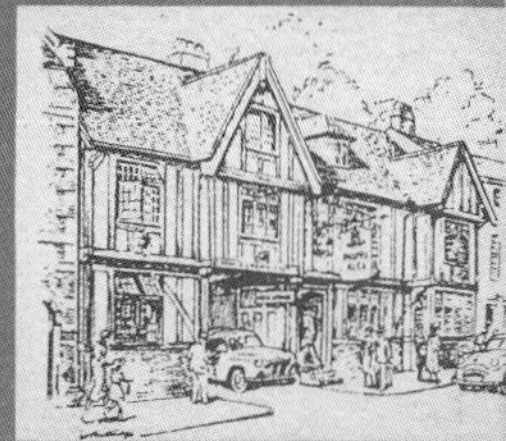

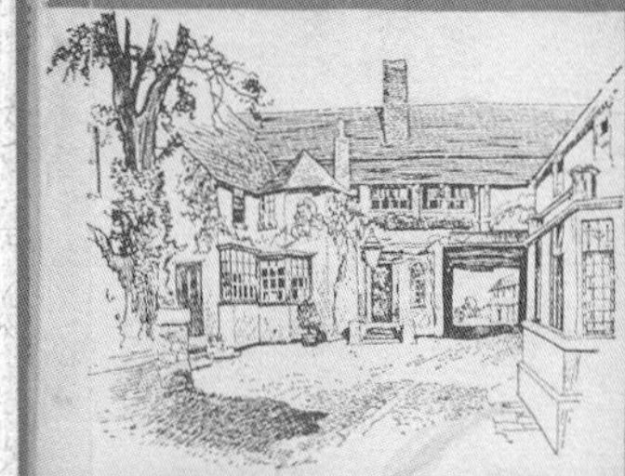

HOSTELRIES OF CHARACTER

in which to

DINE, DRINK & DALLY

fully described by

Peter Stanley Williams

SECOND EDITION

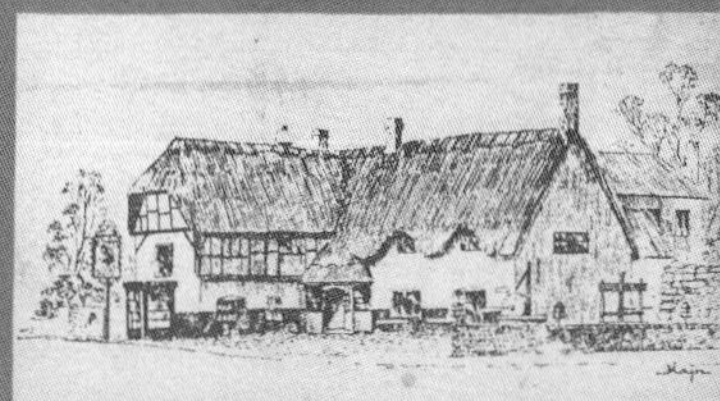

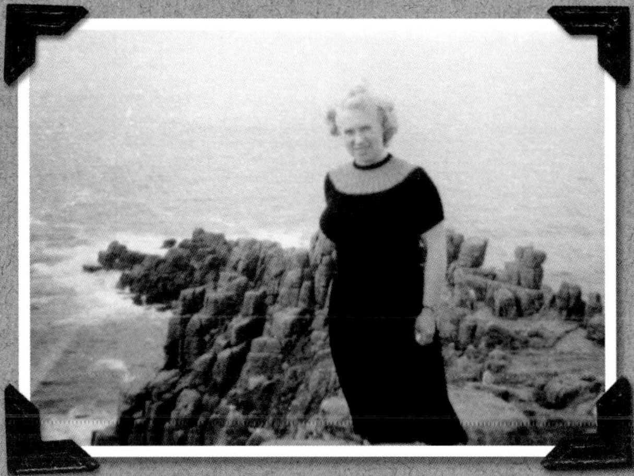

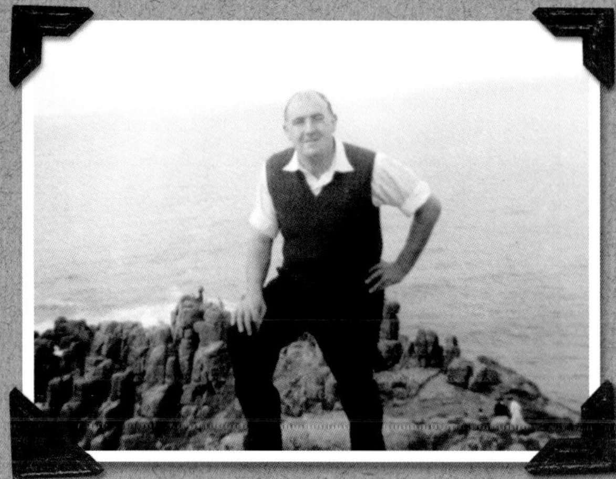

Beryl and Maurice eventually retired to Kingsteignton, near Newton Abbot in Devon, where they enjoyed many happy years together and continued to explore their favourite places (and pubs!) around Devon and Cornwall.

Afterword

Beryl Rabbitts was born at Portsmouth in 1927, the daughter of a Naval Officer. She was brought up in Reading, Berkshire, where she met Maurice Hayward at school. They started 'going out' when she was 13. Maurice was two years older and they married in 1947. Beryl had a younger brother, John, and Maurice was an only child.

B & M never had children, which left them free to enjoy their favourite pastimes of driving and visiting pubs, a mix which isn't encouraged today! That said, they always had a full no claims bonus. 'B' worked full time in an accounts office and 'M' was a bicycle sales rep. Almost every night of the week they would come home from work, change, and drive out for the evening, usually visiting two or three pubs minimum. Dinner was not until arriving back home around 11pm, and usually consisted of steak, chips, sausage, bacon etc etc! It was no surprise that their cat, Rusty, weighed in at an impressive 2 stone, which earned him the front page of a local Reading newspaper.

At one time B & M stayed with Beryl's brother John and his wife Mollie for several weeks, while waiting to move into a new house. Did they change their lifestyle? Of course not! They were to be found in my mother's kitchen late almost every night, frying up after returning from their evening out. Not a nice smell wafting upstairs at that time of the day as I well recall. I'm not sure if they did the washing up. I must remember to ask my mother. Holidays were always taken at home. 'B' didn't like boats and 'M' was afraid of flying. They mainly travelled around Cornwall, Devon, The Lake

District and Scotland. Two week trips to Scotland usually involved about 3000 miles, such was their enjoyment of driving.

B & M's lifestyle did not change over some 50 years and they were well known to pub landlords far and wide. They were as happy and devoted a couple as you will find and they lived a long and healthy life together. In 52 years of marriage they didn't spend a single night apart. To say they dressed smartly to go out for the evening is an understatement and in later years they had a new car every year, often a Jaguar.

Maurice died in 2000, and Beryl passed away in 2006, when these diaries were discovered and some extracts read at her funeral.

Their other true love was Cornwall and upon Beryl's death their ashes were scattered together in the sea off St Mawes, overlooking Falmouth harbour - their favourite spot.

And yes, their ashes really did blow back all over me - but I didn't mind.

Bob Kabbillo

(Beryl's nephew)

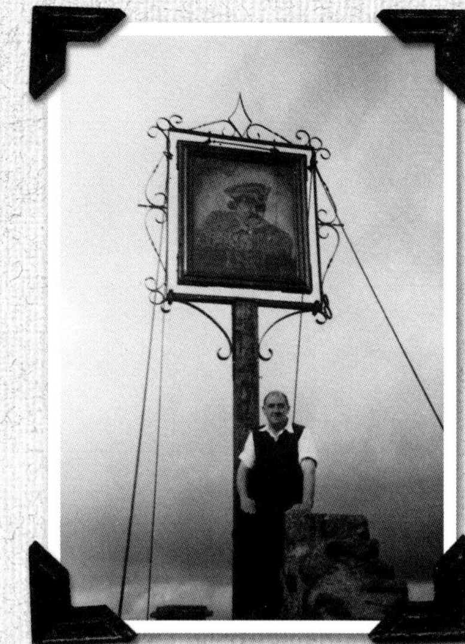

ISBN 978 185022 229 3

Published by Truran, Goonance, Water Lane, St Agnes, Cornwall TR5 0RA
www.truranbooks.co.uk

Truran is an imprint of Truran Books Ltd

Designed by Alix Wood; www.alixwood.co.uk

Printed and bound in Cornwall by R Booth Ltd, The Praze, Penryn, Cornwall TR10 8AA